MW01243818

MS. CHEAP'S Guide To NASHVILLE

The Best Nashville Has to Offer...at a Discount!

MARY HANCE

RUTLEDGE HILL PRESS®
Nashville, Tennessee

Published in Nashville, Tennessee, by Rutledge Hill Press, 211 Seventh Avenue North, Nashville, Tennessee 37219.

Distributed in Canada by H. B. Fenn & Company, Ltd., 34 Nixon Road, Bolton, Ontario L7E 1W2.

Distributed in Australia by The Five Mile Press Pty., Ltd., 22 Summit Road, Noble Park, Victoria 3174.

Distributed in New Zealand by Tandem Press, 2 Rugby Road, Birkenhead, Auckland 10.

Distributed in the United Kingdom by Verulam Publishing, Ltd., 152a Park Street Lane, Park Street, St. Albans, Hertfordshire AL2 2AU.

Inside celebrity photos: Bill Cody, courtesy of TNN; Jeannie Seely, courtesy of Jeannie Seely; Porter Wagoner, courtesy of Porter Wagoner Enterprises; Jo Dee Messina, by Randee St. Nicholas and courtesy of Starstruck Entertainment; Mark O'Connor, by Krisstoffersen and courtesy of Network Ink; Jan Howard, courtesy of Grand Ole Opry; and George Lindsey, courtesy of Top Billing.

Cover and page design by Holland Design Communication.

Cover and clip art by Wes Ware Illustration.

Typography by E. T. Lowe, Nashville, TN.

Library of Congress Cataloging-in-Publication Data

Hance, Mary, 1953–
    Ms. Cheap's guide to Nashville / Mary Hance.
     Rev. ed
      p.   cm.
     ISBN 1-55853-709-0 (pbk.)
     1. Nashville (Tenn.) — Guidebooks.   I. Title.
F444.N23H36   1997
917-68'550453—dc21   97-3379
                                                                          CIP

Printed in the United States of America

1 2 3 4 5 6 7 8 9—02 01 00 99 98

To my parents, Virginia and Brinkley Morton,
for helping me learn the value of money;

To my husband, Bill,
for supporting me in the writing of this book;

And to our daughters, Elizabeth and Anna,
who are (hopefully) learning the value of money.

I want to especially thank my editors at, first,
the *Nashville Banner* and now the *Tennessean* for
allowing me to be Ms. Cheap and to write about
frugal things in our daily newspaper.

Contents

Introduction

Hello, all you thrifty people! Welcome to Nashville, otherwise affectionately known as Music City. Whether you are vacationing, visiting here on business, or already living in the Nashville area—and unless you live on a permanent expense account—*this is the book for you.*

I've lived here more than twenty years, and I have spent all that time working as a newspaper reporter. That, as you might have heard, puts me in the class of people not especially known for making a lot of money. By the very nature of who we are and what we do for a living, we are by necessity frugal. I'm cheap and proud of it. Around town, they call me "Ms. Cheap," thanks to my *Tennessean* column of the same name. My column focuses on all kinds of good deals around Nashville and the midstate—cheap restaurants, great sales, bargain basements, how to save on weddings, how to cut costs on parties, how to tell when you are being gypped, how to recognize value . . . on and on. Believe me, I never run out of things on the subject of frugality about which to write.

Ms. Cheap's theory is simple: Whatever you are buying, I'll bet you can buy it more cheaply. How? Just think ahead; do some research before you head out with wallet and checkbook in hand. Then there's my favorite—*bargain* with the salesperson. Here in Music City, you don't have to pay top dollar for everything. I'll show you in this book how to do it—how to get the most for your money. Visitors to Nashville can let this book be their tour guide. Likewise, almost everything contained in *Ms. Cheap's Guide to Nashville* will fascinate permanent residents here as they discover exciting, new ways to stretch the budget!

You will find out how to get discounts at attractions such as the Nashville Zoo, the Cumberland Science Museum, and hotels and motels. You'll find out where to shop for the best values at malls, shops, and consignment stores. There's also a list of cheap places to eat, play, and visit, as well as a list of 101 things that are absolutely free in and around Nashville. And, of course, there's more, much more. You will find some repetition, as the same information appears in different sections where applicable.

Nashville, Tennessee: It's a great city with lots to do. Enjoy yourself. But don't go home broke.

Finally, I welcome all suggestions and tips for staying cheap in Nashville. Please mail to me your own information for possible inclusion in future editions of *Ms. Cheap's Guide to Nashville.* The mailing address is Ms. Cheap, c/o the *Tennessean,* 1100 Broadway, Nashville, Tennessee 37203. She can be e-mailed at www.mscheapɑtennessean.com.

NOTE: All the information contained in this book—telephone numbers, addresses, and prices—were current as of April 1998, to the best of my knowledge.

Ms. Cheap

Getting Started

Nashville is blessed with a very reliable chamber of commerce. Unfortunately, there is no 800 number (they are cheap . . . er, thrifty . . . too) but you can write the Nashville Area Chamber of Commerce and receive a packet of good information and even a coupon book. The address is Convention and Visitors Bureau, 161 Fourth Avenue North, Nashville, Tennessee 37219. If you must call, the number is 615-259-4700. (Turn to this book's last page for a handy order form.)

Ask for the *Nashville Music City Vacation Guide*. It has everything you might want—information on accommodations, attractions, restaurants, shopping, maps, etc., all in one booklet. Although this guide is clearly designed for tourists, newcomers want and need a lot of the same information. Be sure to ask for the coupon book that is good for all kinds of discounts on Nashville's places of interest, as well as a few restaurants and motels.

NASHVILLE CELEBRITY INSIDER'S TIP

WSM deejay Bill Cody: "A family tradition at our house is for my son and me on Saturday morning to go to the breakfast bar at Arby's. It's $2.99 and we just embarrass ourselves. We go to the one at I-40 and Mount Juliet Road.

"I also love LaBamba Mexican Restaurant (2416 Lebanon Road). It is a lot for a little at lunch or dinner.

"I love bookstores and I love Books-A-Million. I have that Millionaire's Discount Card and it is

(Continued on next page)

Convention and Visitors Bureau officials suggest that if there is something out of the ordinary that you would like to explore (e.g., canoeing, hang-gliding, etc.), let them know and they will send along information on that, too.

In addition to the chamber's bureau, you should also contact Greater Nashville Regional Council at 501 Union Street, 6th Floor, Nashville, Tennessee 37219-1705, or call 615-862-8828. The council has a nifty brochure that describes and maps out eighty-four points of interest in the midstate.

Once you are here:

1. Your first stop should be the Visitors Information Center situated in the Nashville Arena on Broadway at Fifth Avenue South. This little hospitality hub is chock-full of information concerning Nashville and the surrounding area. This is *the place* to discover what's happening, when, where, and for how much. It's open seven days a week and has helpful people in addition to all the great reference material. This is also a

good place to collect information to be used for, say, an elementary school social studies project featuring Nashville. 259-4747.

2. Get the scoop on what's up for the current week. The chamber's Nashville Music City USA calendar of events is a good overview, but you need to get the *Tennessean* (seven days a week, in the A.M., which sell for 50¢ apiece ($1.75 on Sunday) and the *Nashville Scene,* which is free. Those two publications together will give you the latest on clubs, music, entertainment, family outings, etc. The *Scene* comes out on Wednesdays. The *Tennessean* gives good entertainment information in its Sunday Showcase and Friday Weekend sections.

great. For music, go to Compact Discovery. In addition to being really reasonably priced, with every twelfth CD you buy, you get one free.

"My son is a card collector and there is a place called Carl's Cards next to T J Maxx in Hickory Hollow that has the best in town.

"A great bargain is college football. And the best college football for the money is at Sewanee (the University of the South, which is about ninety miles from Nashville). It's great."

3. If you happen to be among those folks who have recently moved to town or to another area in town, one of your first calls should be to the Welcome Wagon. A courteous and knowledgeable person will visit you and bring you all kinds of goodies. When my family and I moved across town recently, Welcome Wagon brought us half of a pound cake and a basket full of coupons for everything ranging from dry cleaning to picture framing to haircuts. The coupons are from merchants in your new neighborhood, so not only do you get the discounts but also an easy way to find the services you need. This is not just for homeowners.

Welcome Wagon also visits newcomers in apartments. Call 883-9521 if you're in Middle Tennessee; otherwise (800) 779-3526.

The Nashville Arena symbolizes continued growth in the city's commitment to arts, entertainment, and sports. At this writing, Nashville was preparing to welcome its National Hockey League franchise, which would call the arena home. (Dane Herndon)

Ways to Save Money on Your Nashville Trip

1. **Make your trip in the winter.** Tourism officials say that during January and February, rooms can cost only half of what the going rate is for the peak summer season.

2. **Search out the limited-service hotels or hotels in the outlying areas.** The Harding Place/I-24 area often has some bargains. Try to find one that has free local calls so that you can check out current happenings and discounts from the convenience of your room.

3. **Look for entertainment deals**—that is, places where there is no cover charge or where the cover doesn't kick in until late at night. There are specials such as writers' nights and jam sessions. Don't be shy: It's okay to call the club and find out how the cover works. Furthermore, there is plenty of free music available in some of the lounges on Lower Broadway, at the Opryland Hotel, other hotel lounges, at writers' nights, jam sessions, and coffee houses. The newspapers' entertainment sections are a good source on what's current. Better yet, stay tuned here for some ideas in Ms. Cheap's list of "101 Free Things" to do.

4. **Seek out promotions and use the coupons.** Most tourist attractions have all kind of discounts. Call your desired destination first to inquire about any specials or deals. Look for coupons—there are those that offer

20 percent off at a restaurant, or buy one entrée and get the second one free. There's also 10 percent off for early birds. These deals are in the newspapers, as well as in the chamber's coupon book available at the information center at the Nashville Arena, mall management offices, etc.

5. **There are a couple of discount packages you may want to invest in** (if you are going to be here long enough)—the *Entertainment Book,* which is an inch-thick book that has coupons for everything from hotels, to restaurants, to attractions, to dry cleaning, to photo developing. It goes for $30, with some of the proceeds benefiting local nonprofits. While thirty bucks might sound like a lot of cash to part with, you will be amazed at how quickly this book pays for itself with perks such as buy-one-get-one-free deals at fancy restaurants as well as fast-food joints. In fact, dozens of Nashville-area attractions of all types offer discounts through these coupons. This book would be a good investment for newcomers who want to get to know a lot of places, or even for the visitor or tourist spending a week here and looking for all kinds of neat things to do and places at which to eat. Call 833-4920 to find out what nonprofit organizations are selling it or to buy one direct.

    The second bargain also benefits nonprofits and schools and involves a Smart Discount Card ($6). They are the size of a credit card and are good for price cuts at restaurants, on soft drinks, for dry cleaning, on pizza deals, etc. They're issued each August by a company called Innovative Funding and are good for a year. To get one for yourself, call area schools to see if they are selling them. If that doesn't work, call Second Harvest Food Bank at 329-3491.

6. **Check out the festivals and events** here and in the surrounding counties. Most are free, or at least reasonable, and involve music, entertainment, people-watching, and lots of fun. For a calendar of events, call the Tourist Information Center at 259-4747, or the Tennessee Department of Tourist Development at 741-2158. The Greater Nashville Regional Council also has a calendar that includes many festivals and events in the midstate—call 862-8828.

7. **Look for packages,** such as those through Opryland Hotel or Gray Line. Many times you get more for your money if you can be included in a package. Some include accommodations and some don't.

8. **Be reasonable about what and where you eat.** It's easy to blow your vacation budget on food without even really enjoying it. Nashville is blessed with oodles of great and reasonably priced restaurants where you can soak up some local color to go with the great food. Consult Ms. Cheap's list of restaurants (chapter 7) where you can eat for about $6 a person, tops.

9. **Seek out the cheap parking on the fringes of downtown or use the trolley** instead of parking downtown. Either can save you a lot and make things more convenient, too. During the peak season, the trolley runs every twenty minutes, and it links parking to Second Avenue as well as Music Row.

10. **Buy *Ms. Cheap's Guide to Nashville*** and use all of her tips. (After all, you do want me to be thorough in making this list as good as it can be, right?)

t   w   o

Lodging

Finding a reasonable place to stay might be a challenge. But you should have your copy of the *Nashville Music City Vacation Guide* that was sent to you by the Convention and Visitors Bureau (surely, you remembered to call or write ahead). It has a complete listing of hotels, motels, bed and breakfasts, and camping options.

Campgrounds

Obviously, camping would be the cheapest overnight option, with some campsites charging as little as $10 per night. More good news: There are six campgrounds in the immediate Nashville area. Some, like the giant Opryland KOA and the lakefront Hermitage Landing RV Resort, have cabins as well as campsites.

Opryland KOA really has a lot to offer, with free country music shows every night and a swimming pool that is open March through October. This KOA campground on Music Valley Drive is just a few minutes from the Opryland Hotel and has 460 spaces. The twenty-five cabins, some of which sleep as many as six people, offer electricity, heat, and air conditioning. You have to bring your own sheets or sleeping bags. Each cabin has a grill, just like the more basic campsites, and, of course, everyone has access to the community showers and bath facilities. For peak times such as Fan Fair, campsites are booked as far as a year and a half out, but during most of the year, there are sites available for reservation. Another plus for the Opryland KOA is its $3 shuttle that runs between the hotel and the campground. The $3 fee gives you shuttle access for your entire stay.

Hermitage Landing is another good bet. It is situated on J. Percy Priest Lake and comes complete with twenty cabins and 156 campsites. These cabins have indoor plumbing, supply bedsheets, sleep up to six, and rent for $60 a night. The setting is beautiful, particularly for water lovers, but it is not as close to the other attractions as is Opryland KOA or some of the other camping facilities. Hermitage Landing is just off Interstate 40 at the 221B exit.

Hotels and Motels

These choices are a lot more varied, with prices ranging from around $50 a night to $160 a night. The best rates generally are on the fringes or just outside of the city. But in the city itself, and even in the popular Opryland area, there are plenty of budget and economy limited-service options.

"The limited-service hotels are great," says Butch Spyridon, executive director of the Nashville Convention and Visitors Bureau. "And prices can be great during the winter months, particularly in the outlying communities."

Spyridon says to try the Harding Place/I-24 area, where prices seem to be pretty modest. If you need help, call the bureau. "We try to stay out of recommending places, but if they say, 'I only have $40,' we will try to help them," Spyridon adds.

Even the expensive places have deals. You just have to play your cards right and do a little research.

"A lot of people don't realize that if you are flexible, you can save a ton of money," says Sandy Stuckey, who supervises special promotions at the Opryland Hotel, where rack rates are the highest in the city. In some cases—with the right planning or package—you can get a room at something approaching half the rack rate price. But you have to ask and maybe even be a little creative.

"Ask if they have a honeymoon package," says Stuckey. "You don't have to be on your honeymoon. If you call a hotel and tell them it is a special occasion, a lot of them will upgrade you if they are full. It doesn't hurt to ask if there is a chance of an upgrade. They would rather upgrade somebody who is celebrating a special occasion than somebody just walking through the door."

Stuckey also advises savvy hotel shoppers to think about what seasons are the slowest for hotels and book during those times (in Opryland's case, that's the first quarter of the year).

■ **Ms. Cheap's Quick-Saving Tip:**

Patronize motels that have free local calls and free breakfast. The breakfast deal can be a wonderful freebie, especially if you're traveling as a family.

The other trick is getting in on a package. For example, at Christmas, Opryland Hotel has a three-night holiday package that includes a dinner show, a cruise on the *General Jackson*, tickets to the crafts fair, and other goodies for considerably less than three nights' lodging at the rack rate. By the way, most of the larger hotels have some sort of package, so ask.

The number of bed and breakfasts in the Nashville area has increased to around fifteen, and they can be reasonable or quite expensive, depending on the place and the demand. If this is the way you want to go, the chamber guide has a list from which you can choose. It might be a bargain, but don't just assume a bed and breakfast would necessarily be a cheap route for you.

The General Jackson *riverboat cruises the Cumberland River.* (Nashville Convention and Visitors Bureau)

"Top Ten"
Special Lodging Suggestions

Truth be told, it's really difficult to mention "cheap" and "lodging" in the same sentence, unless you're talking about campgrounds, really cheap motels, or even abandoned buildings. But in a day and age where many travelers don't balk at $200-a-night accommodations, you don't have to spend hundreds of dollars for a hotel room in Nashville. There are lots of good deals on nice clean hotel and motel rooms. Remember this: if you can get a decent family-sized room priced nightly in the double digits, you are living cheaply. Besides, most of these places allow children under eighteen to stay free in their parents' rooms. And be sure to ask about AAA, AARP, or senior discounts, and if they apply. The following rates listed apply most of the year, although special Nashville events such as Fan Fair will drive prices up. Again, call ahead.

Here are the best bets:

1. **AmeriSuites** has two locations—one at 220 Rudy Circle (615-872-0422) and one in Brentwood at 202 Summit View Drive (615-661-9477). Both can be reached by calling 1-800-833-1516. Prices in Brentwood start at $88 for a double. All of the rooms are suites with refrigerator, microwave, and coffee maker. Free continental breakfast daily. At Rudy Circle, prices start at $98 for a double.

2. **Courtyard by Marriott** has three locations, one at 2508 Elm Hill Pike (615-883-9500), another in Brentwood at 103 East Park Drive (371-9200), and one near

Vanderbilt University at 1901 West End Avenue (615-327-9900). They can be reached at 1-800-321-2211. Rates for a double start at $85 a night and go up to $125.

3. **Days Inn** has a number of locations. Two of the best offerings are the one near Vanderbilt, at 1800 West End Avenue, and another near the airport, at 1 International Plaza and Briley Parkway. The airport location's direct number is 615-361-7666. Rates start at $39 and go up to $79. The airport hotel is older but was renovated in 1993. The Days Inn Vanderbilt has a direct number, 615-327-0922. Double rates start at $69 a night. Free breakfast. The 800 number for both is 1-800-851-1962.

4. **Econo Lodge,** 2460 Music Valley Drive (615-889-0090 or 1-800-553-2666). The rates are anywhere from $52 to $70 a night for double occupancy.

5. **Guesthouse/MedCenter Inn,** 1909 Hayes Street (615-329-1000 or 1-800-777-4904). Doubles begin at $59 a night, and there is free continental breakfast and twenty-four-hour coffee service. Also, all rooms offer microwaves and refrigerators.

6. **Hampton Inns has six Nashville-area locations,** any of which would be good. The 800 number is

1-800-HAMPTON. Prices vary among the properties but some (such as the one on Brick Church Pike) start as low as $54 a night. Most start in the $65-to-$75 range and offer a free breakfast as well as free local calls, pool, etc.

7. **Inn at Opryland**, across from Opryland Hotel (615-889-0800). This is not rock bottom on the prices, but it is a nice property and is owned by Opryland Hotel. There is a free shuttle to the Opryland Hotel and airport. The double room prices range from $66 in the dead of winter to $99 in the summer months. Indoor pool.

8. **The two Shoney's Inns** are good prospects for location and price. One is located at 2420 Music Valley Drive (615-885-4030, 1-800-222-2222). The other is at 1521 Demonbreun Street, right in the middle of Music Row (615-255-9977). Both start at just over $70 for a double. Free continental breakfast, free local calls. There is even an indoor heated swimming pool at the Opryland location.

9. **A Homeplace in Nolensville** is a very well-regarded bed and breakfast. It is located about twenty minutes from downtown. The owners, Alfred and Evelyn Bennett, have three rooms and a cottage that rents by the night or by the week. Homeplace rates range from $50 to $75 a night. 615-776-5181.

10. **Fredda Odom's Bed and Breakfast Hospitality International** offers a good way to get a bed and breakfast room, with a reservation service. Odom is based in Nashville but is the link to more than one

hundred B&Bs in the state as well as others around the world. Prices range from $55 a night to $150 a night in most cases. Call 615-331-5244 for information or reservations. Odom has a brochure that includes many of the Tennessee options.

3
t h r e e

101 Free Things

Okay, here we go with what you've been waiting for (offered in no particular order of preference):

1. Tour Opryland Hotel. Your self-guided tour around this virtual city-within-the-city could take up the better part of a day if you really take it all in: the Conservatory, the Cascades, and the new Delta interior gardens. There are beautifully landscaped walkways and the temperature is always a pleasant seventy degrees. Seeing is believing here. Hotel parking is $5. 889-1000.

2. Enjoy the free music at night in all of Opryland Hotel's lounges. Choose from the Stagedoor Lounge, the Pickin' Parlor, Jack Daniel Saloon, and the Delta Lounge. On any given night, each lounge has a pretty decent band. With four choices, you can bet on something worth listening to. Remember, this is, after all, *Music City*. So much fine talent has started at Opryland that you might just see the next Vince Gill or whomever. Be sure to arrange your schedule so that you can enjoy Vince Cardell on the piano and the dancing waters in the Cascades at 7:00 and 9:00 every night. It is a great show—about thirty minutes in length—featuring Cardell's piano music as well as an impressive light and water show. This is particularly striking around Christmas, but it's also very crowded. If you are going during the holidays, call Opryland for a complete schedule of free things to do in the hotel. Hotel parking is $5. 889-1000.

3. The Grand Ole Opry museum is free and very interesting. However, you had better go soon, because it probably won't always be free. The museum pays tribute to Country Music Hall of Fame members and Opry stars with extensive exhibits. Parking is $2. 889-6611.

4. Get free line dancing lessons for the whole family from the pros at the Wildhorse Saloon (120 Second Avenue North) every day from 4:00 P.M. until 9:00 P.M. and 1:00 P.M. until 9:00

■ *Ms. Cheap's Quick-Saving Tip:*

Don't speed. It's a lot cheaper to go slower than the speed limit and thus not get a ticket.

P.M. in the peak season. It's thirty minutes of lessons and thirty minutes of dancing, and it's completely free if you get there before 5:00 P.M. If you just want to watch the dancin' and carryin' on, that's okay, too. But get there before 5:00 P.M. if you want to get in before the cover charge kicks in.

The Grand Ole Opry. Of course, this is the main entertainment venue that brings country music fans to Nashville. Several museums in proximity offer convenient sidelights. (Donnie Beauchamp photo, courtesy of Nashville Convention and Visitors Bureau)

The cover is $3 on weeknights and $6 on weekends, and even a little more when there is special entertainment. Call the hot line at 256-WILD to get a recorded message of what's happening, or call 251-1000 for direct information.

5. Attend a free taping of *Prime Time Country*, hosted by Gary Chapman. The show tapes at 5:00 P.M. on weekdays at Studio A of the Opry House at Opryland. Doors open at 4:00 P.M. Tickets are free, but you must call

for reservations, 889-6611. Parking is $2 in the Opryland parking lot.

6. Attend a taping at TNN (The Nashville Network). Some are free and some are not, so be sure to know which is which. There are periodic free tapings on the CMT Monday Night Concerts at the Ryman Auditorium, with top stars such as Wynonna, Vince Gill, and Pam Tillis performing. Other options include the *Charlie Daniels' Talent Roundup, Ralph Emery on the Record,* and the *Statler Brothers Show,* all of which are free. For information on these and other periodic free tapings, call 883-7000 and ask what tapings are coming up and how to get in. Most require reservations, so be sure to call.

7. Visit Hatch Showprint at 316 Broadway, the oldest known poster shop in America. Hatch has been in business since 1879 and did printing work for

Ryman Auditorium. (Donnie Beauchamp photo, courtesy of Nashville Convention and Visitors Bureau)

vaudeville, circuses, musical events, sporting events, etc., and was the printer of choice for Grand Ole Opry stars. It's open Monday through Saturday from 10:00 A.M. until 5:30 P.M., and you can walk in and see the same techniques being used today that were used as far back as the fifteenth century. These days Hatch is doing work for contemporary artists. Call to find out about Sunday hours. 256-2805.

8. Tour the Tennessee State Capitol, which was designed by noted architect William Strickland. It is situated on Charlotte Avenue between Sixth and Seventh Avenues, and it has self-guided walking tour brochures at the information desk. The capitol, which took more than fifteen years to build and was completed in 1859, is pretty much as it originally was constructed. The first-floor hallway, the library, and supreme court chamber all have been restored

Tennessee State Capitol at night.
(Nashville Convention and Visitors Bureau)

to their nineteenth-century appearance. The style is Greek Ionic. Interestingly, Strickland died during the construction and is buried in the northeast corner. Also buried on the grounds is James K. Polk (the eleventh U.S. president). The state capitol grounds is also the site for an Andrew Jackson monument that stands near the east entrance portico as a tribute to the nation's seventh president and hero of the battle of New Orleans. Hours are 9:00 A.M. to 4:00 P.M., Monday through Friday. 741-2692 or 741-1621.

9. Visit the Tennessee State Museum, at 505 Deaderick Street. Occasionally, there is a charge for special exhibits, but on most days this great downtown museum of Tennessee history is completely free. The museum, a collection of history-related materials through the nineteenth century, is in the James K. Polk Building downtown. There is a large collection focused on prehistoric Indians and an emphasis on the Civil War. It is open from 10:00 A.M. to 5:00 P.M., Tuesday through Saturday, and from 1:00 to 5:00 P.M. on Sunday. 741-2692.

10. Visit the Upper Room Chapel and Museum, at 1908 Grand Avenue, near Vanderbilt University. The chapel features an eight-by-seventeen-foot wood carving of the Last Supper, which was copied from Leonardo da Vinci's painting, and an eight-by-twenty-foot stained-glass window with the Pentecost theme. The museum has religious art dating from 1300 to 1990. There are seasonal displays of one hundred Nativity scenes. Hours are 8:00 A.M. to 4:30 P.M., Monday through Friday. The chapel is, technically, free but they encourage a donation. 340-7207.

11. Go on the Nashville Citywalk, the walking tour of downtown. Since its debut in 1994, the blue-lined route has been drawing tourists, natives, and those who work downtown to highlights of the city. Designed by the Metro

Historical Commission, the tour starts at Fort Nashborough, which is a re-creation of Nashville's original settlement on the Cumberland River. The walk extends two miles down Second Avenue and through Printers Alley. It winds past the state capitol, several historic churches, a historic black business district on Fourth Avenue, the refurbished Ryman Auditorium, and the Hermitage Hotel.

The Citywalk also passes the Hard Rock Cafe, Tootsie's Orchid Lounge, and Planet Hollywood on Broadway. Modeled after the Freedom Trail in Boston, Citywalk also includes sheet metal silhouettes of figures in historical dress and historical markers at points of interest. Historical Commission staff members researched photo files for accurate references on the silhouettes, which range from a communicant at Saint Mary's Church to the sax player and newsboy in Printers Alley. To get a map/brochure, write the Metro Historical Commission, 209 10th Avenue South, Nashville, Tennessee 37203, or call 862-7970, or drop by the Visitors Center in the Nashville Arena.

12. Tour Fort Nashborough. Fort Nashborough's replica is on the river on First Avenue North, between Church and Broadway. The original Fort Nashborough was larger, covering two acres, and stood about five hundred yards west of the replica. It was a log stockade built in 1780 by settlers seeking protection from Creek and Cherokee Indians. James Robertson and John Donelson, leaders of the settlement, named it Nashborough in honor of their friend Francis Nash, a North Carolina Revolutionary War general killed in 1777. In 1780 the Cumberland Compact was signed at the fort, establishing the settlement and its government. The fort, operated by Metro Parks, is on the self-guided walking tour of downtown Nashville. There is no admission charge, and the fort is open from 8:30 A.M. to 4:30 P.M., Monday through Saturday. 862-8400.

13. Take the walking tour of Mount Olivet Cemetery, 1101 Lebanon Road. The cemetery offers the free tour Monday through Saturday from 8:30 A.M. to 5:00 P.M. It also may be followed by car. Visitors are asked to check in at the funeral home before getting started. Local historian Ridley Wills has written the book *Walking Tour* ($5.95) that can serve as a handy guide. The walking tour of Mount Olivet is a self-guided, moderate, mile-and-a-half trek that follows along the top of a hill. An audio cassette narrated by Wills follows the outline of his book and may be checked out for free at the Mount Olivet Funeral Home for the driving tour.

Included among the landmarks are a replica of Napoleon's tomb (Paris) at the Vernon K. Stevenson crypt in Nashville; two sphinxes guarding the pyramid-shaped tomb of Eugene C. Lewis, who in 1896 came up with the idea to build the Parthenon for the state's centennial celebration; a Celtic cross marking the grave of Anne Dallas Dudley, a leading Tennessee suffragist who rallied the state to ratify the Nineteenth Amendment, becoming the "perfect thirty-six"; an opulent statue of Jesus Christ with three children, commemorating the Warner family that lost three of their children to cholera during a one-year span; and a forty-five-foot-tall obelisk, topped with a nine-foot-tall statue of a Confederate soldier, as a memorial to the nearly fifteen hundred Confederates buried here. 255-4193.

14. Even older is the Nashville City Cemetery, the only Tennessee cemetery listed on the National Register of Historic Places. Located on Fourth Avenue South at Oak Street, this cemetery was closed in 1878 with twenty-three thousand graves in it. The gates are open from 7:30 A.M. until dusk. It is known for the architectural distinction of some of its monuments as well as for its historical significance. There are hundreds of Union soldiers buried here.

For information, call the Metro Historical Commission at 862-7970.

15. Take a walk through the Bicentennial Capitol Mall State Park downtown. Completed in June 1996, the mall is an outdoor museum with a walking history of the state and its ninety-five counties. One of the highlights is a 250-foot granite map of the state. There are also thirty-one fountains representing the state's major rivers and what is said to be the nation's largest carillon (a set of bells, sounded by hammers and controlled by a keyboard). The nineteen-acre state park is next to Farmers Market between Jefferson Street and James Robertson Parkway, north of the capitol. 741-5280.

16. Take the self-guided driving tour of the Civil War battle of Nashville. This tour includes the main points of the Union defenses of Nashville and the Confederate lines on the first and second days of the battle, which occurred in December 1864. It was considered one of the most decisive battles of the war. 862-7970, or call the Convention and Visitors Bureau at 251-4747.

17. Visit the midstate Civil War battlefields. One is Fort Donelson National Battlefield in Dover, the site of the 1862 battle that opened up the Cumberland and Tennessee Rivers to Union domination. Fort Donelson is on National Cemetery Drive in Dover, which is about an hour and a half away, northwest of Nashville. Another nearby Civil War site is the Stones River National Battlefield and Cemetery on Old Nashville Highway in Murfreesboro, where one of the bloodiest battles of the war was fought in 1862 and 1863. 893-9501.

18. Tour the Governor's Mansion, 882 South Curtiswood Lane. The governor's residence was built between 1929 and 1931 and purchased by the state in 1948. It is open for tours, March through December, on Tuesdays and

Thursdays from 10:00 A.M. until noon. Groups of five or more should call for reservations. The tour takes about thirty minutes. 383-5401.

19. Visit the Museum of Tobacco Art and History at the corner of Eighth Avenue North and Harrison Street. The four-thousand-square-foot museum is the only one of its kind in North America and features a variety of antiques that are associated with tobacco, pipes that are as much as one thousand years old, wooden cigar store figures, snuff boxes, cigar holders, etc. U.S. Tobacco purchased the collection in the early 1980s from an Englishman and established the museum in the U.S. Tobacco complex. The museum, which also has an interesting gift shop, is just across from the Bicentennial Mall and the new Farmers Market. Admission is free and there is free parking across the street. Hours are 9:00 A.M. to 4:00 P.M. 271-2349.

20. Walk through the Arcade in the middle of downtown Nashville. The Arcade, which runs from Fourth to Fifth Avenue between Church and Union Streets, was Nashville's first shopping center when it opened just after the turn of the century. The two-story Greek Revival structure was built in 1903 and now houses shops and restaurants. It was built as a replica of an arcade in Milan, Italy. Nowadays it is a collection of restaurants and a few shops, and it is full of activity during weekday lunch hours. It is open weekdays 6:00 A.M. through 6:00 P.M. 255-1034.

21. Take a walking tour of the Vanderbilt University campus. Since Vanderbilt's founding in 1873, trees and the campus landscape have been important, as I'll explain here in just a second. There is a walking tour map that charts tours of the old campus and Peabody campus, pointing out exterior sculpture and art work and identifying more than sixty campus trees. Vanderbilt gained arboretum status in 1988 and boasts several state champion trees, which are the largest officially recognized specimens of their species in Tennessee. Don't miss the Bicentennial Oak, which is certified to have been growing on its own since before the Revolutionary War.

The tour maps are popular with prospective students and their parents, as well as with scout leaders and schoolteachers who bring their troops and classes to study campus trees. To get a tour map, see the university receptionist on the second floor of Kirkland Hall (historic building with clock tower). Or call the PR office at 322-2706 to get a copy sent. (Multiple copies cost 75¢ but single copies are free.)

22. Not many people know this, but every Friday at 5:00 P.M. there is **a tour of the historic Union Station Hotel.** The concierge leads guests and the general public on a fifteen-minute walk through the hotel and talks about the hotel's history and its Romanesque Revival architecture. The hotel even serves refreshments (cookies and lemonade or hot chocolate) at the end of the tour. Tours can also be arranged at other times by calling 726-1001. The hotel, at 1001 Broadway, served as Nashville's train station for the first three-quarters of the century. It was converted and reopened as a hotel in 1986. The lobby with its marble floors, stained glass, and barrel-vaulted ceiling, and the 222-foot-tall clock tower overlooking downtown are among the highlights.

23. Ellington Agricultural Center's Oscar Farris Agricultural Museum is an interesting outing. The museum contains various household tools and farm implements from the early 1800s through the 1930s. There are also three log cabins depicting a pioneer settlement. Museum director Anne Dale says to allow at least an hour for your visit. She says some people stay all day. The agricultural center occupies two hundred acres as part of the estate of financier Rogers Caldwell and houses the

■ *Ms. Cheap's Quick-Saving Tip:*

Watch the newspapers for free activities. There are tons of them if you'll just take the time to look.

Tennessee Department of Agriculture. Although the museum and cabins are the only buildings open to the public, there is a hillside trail available for a short hike that takes you by the Iris Garden and assorted wildflowers. The museum is open from 9:00 A.M. to 4:00 P.M., Monday through Friday. Call to see if there are any special events on the calendar. Ellington can be reached by following Franklin Road to Hogan Road, then look for the signs. 360-0197.

24. Tour Purity Dairies, 360 Murfreesboro Road. This milk plant tour is geared mostly for groups, which get a full-fledged tour led by "Miss Sally," who has been showing people around the milk and ice cream plant for two decades. The groups also get to see a film about milk, starring Sergeant Glory, a.k.a. Jim Varney. Individuals don't get the full "Miss Sally" tour but are welcome to call to see if someone on staff could give them a tour. It is really very interesting to see the milk processed and to see how ice cream is made and packaged. Call and ask for Sue. Group tours, catering to all ages, are booked a month or two in advance. The individual tours are accepted only if the plant can accommodate them. 244-1900.

25. Take a tour of the Nissan Motor Manufacturing plant in Smyrna. Tours that give an overview of the car manufacturing process are offered on Tuesdays at 8:30 A.M., 10:00 A.M., and 1:00 P.M., and on Thursdays at 8:30 A.M. and 10:00 A.M. You must make reservations, and the company suggests making them about three months in advance. Call 459-1444 for information and reservations. The tour lasts about an hour and twenty minutes and includes a fifteen-minute video presentation.

26. The Saturn automobile plant in Spring Hill has four daily tours, Monday through Friday, at 8:30 A.M., 10:00 A.M., 1:00 P.M., and 2:30 P.M. Reservations are needed for the forty-five-minute tours. Children under six not allowed. Arrive twenty minutes early for safety-film viewing. Tours begin at the Welcome Center on Highway 31 in Spring Hill. (800) 326-3321.

27. A tour of the *Tennessean* news operation. These popular tours take you all the way through the *Tennessean* news operation, to the newsrooms, advertising facilities, press room, makeup facilities, etc. The tour, which is available to groups of up to thirty people, lasts about an hour and is conducted on Tuesday and Friday mornings. Participants must be second-graders or older. The tour is free, but you must make a reservation by calling 726-8908. The tours are often booked months ahead, but some dates are available on short notice.

28. Get free dog dips at the Acme Feed Store, 101 Broadway. This old-fashioned feed and seed store is an outing on its own, but if you can time your visit with the summer Saturday morning dog dips, you're in for a double treat. A free flea dip for your dog is available every Saturday from late spring through the summer. There is a big vat for big dogs and a smaller one for the pups. The dogs and their owners line up and the dogs are dipped, then they shake and go on their merry way. While you are there, browse the store, which has just about everything for pets, such as pigs' ears, etc. 255-5641.

29. Take advantage of the free day at the Hermitage: January 8, celebrated as the anniversary of the battle of New Orleans. There is also a discount day on March 15, Andrew Jackson's birthday. The Hermitage, home of Andrew Jackson, is on 650 acres and is visited by 250,000 people a year. Rebuilt in 1835 after a fire, it overlooks spacious, well-manicured grounds and a lush garden. It is open 9:00 A.M. to 5:00 P.M. every day. The standard admission is $9.50 for adults, $7 for seniors, and $4.50 for children. These free days are a great way to see this popular attraction. 889-2941.

The Hermitage II.
(Nashville Convention and Visitors Bureau)

30. Cheekwood, Nashville's Home of Art and Gardens, has an annual free day that is held in the spring. Located in the beautiful Belle Meade area, Cheekwood's galleries and gardens make it one of Nashville's most popular attractions. You will need to call each year in order to find out which day will be free. Cheekwood is located at 1200 Forrest Park Drive. 356-8000.

31. The Tennessee State Fairgrounds Flea Market is a popular free outing where you see almost everything. Held the fourth weekend of every month, it is one of the largest flea markets in the Southeast and has been named one of the top ten flea markets in the country. Sometimes there are more than one thousand dealers on hand. 862-5016.

32. Visit the firehalls. The Metro fire chief's office says you can drop by and the firefighters (if they are not too busy) will show children the equipment. "We love doing this. We do it every day," Chief Buck Dozier says. 862-8585.

33. The Dyer Observatory on Oman Drive off Granny White Pike has free nights where you can use their telescopes to view the night sky. There is also a twenty-minute video or a speaker at each session. The free nights are held once a month, March through November, except for August. The public nights are the only time the public can come to Dyer, which is a research center and part of Vanderbilt University. The observatory has two telescopes, including one that is the largest in the Southeast. For information about special nights, call 373-4897. Vanderbilt also has a campus observatory in the Stevenson Center that offers public viewings.

34. Attend the weekday tapings of the *Crook and Chase* show. The popular television variety show is taped daily, Monday through Friday, from 11:00 A.M. to noon, at the Jim Owens and Associates studios at 1525 McGavock Street, just off Broadway, between downtown and Music Row. You

NASHVILLE CELEBRITY
INSIDER'S TIP

Country Music Star Jeannie Seely says she is frugal: "It's not just for the money but I think you can find more interesting things if you shop places like estate sales. A dining room table, for example. You know it has been loved and cherished. It's like getting something extra from your grandmother. Plus I think things used to be made better.

As far as eating out, Seely says, "I stay on a pretty strict low-fat diet. But if I had to recommend something, it would be

(Continued on next page)

must call ahead for a reservation (a week or more in advance is suggested), but the show is free and lots of fun. Standby seating also is available if the reservations are all taken. Plan to arrive by 10:30 and to stay until a little after noon. 242-8000.

35. Take a self-guided tour at the Market Street Brewery and Public House, 134 Second Avenue North. See how hand-crafted beer is made by the Bohannon Brewing Company. There is no official tour, but the restaurant is glassed so that you can see the process. The restaurant staff is glad to answer questions if you have any. It's open the same hours as the restaurant, 11:00 A.M. to midnight daily. 242-8223.

36. Wait for free day at the Nashville Zoo. Every year on Super Bowl Sunday, the zoo is open to the public for free. If you can't handle that, call the zoo and ask what promotions they have going on. 370-3333.

37. Make the Metro public library your reading head-quarters. Metro has nineteen libraries, including the main

Ben West Library downtown. The system has 780,000 books, with 30 percent being children's books. There are all kinds of programs for adults and children, including free puppet shows, family storytelling nights, and even free Internet access. Free movie rentals are available, good for five days. 862-5800.

38. Take advantage of story hours at branch libraries. Most branches have at least two story hours every week for preschoolers. These are designed to instill in children the love of reading and usually include a story and a related activity. They are all different so it makes sense to try several. Just call the branch or call the children's division for a complete schedule. 862-5785.

39. Join a book club. Virtually all of the big bookstores have one or more book club opportunities for you. Some even have children's book clubs, such as Media Play's Goosebumps Club. Call the stores and ask what clubs they have and how to join.

Logan's Roadhouse. It is the most fun atmosphere and the small filet—you can't find a better steak for the money. They have a lot of variety, too. You don't have to have steak.

"I like Luby's, too, on Music Valley Drive, especially if you are in a hurry. I am a spinach freak. I always get the spinach and I love the selection of salad—pasta salad, fresh fruit salads . . . it's great."

Seely also had two suggestions for entertainment: "One of the most entertaining things for me is to walk up and down Second Avenue and look at the people and in the stores. It is so much fun.

"For someone who likes to participate and doesn't mind being in a loud place, you should go to the Wildhorse. It's great fun. If you have a boring date, go to the Wildhorse. It's so loud you can't talk anyway."

40. Davis-Kidd Booksellers, 4007 Hillsboro Road, in Green Hills has **Kids' Corner** every Saturday morning at 11:00. There is storytelling, reading, or other entertainment geared for young children. It lasts about forty-five minutes and has consistently been really quality time. 385-2645. Barnes & Noble's Cool-Springs store is also a storytelling center for young children, with events scheduled every Monday and Saturday at 10:00 and 11:30 A.M. 377-9979. Books-A-Million, 1789 North Gallatin Road, also has Saturday children's story hours at 10:30 A.M. and 3:00 P.M. 860-3133.

■ *Ms. Cheap's Quick-Saving Tip:*

Form co-ops with friends or neighbors, and share things such as books and magazines.

41. For the adults or the family that enjoys live performances, Davis-Kidd holds a **Writers' Night** every Friday at 7:30 featuring four or five writers performing their work. It lasts until 9:30 or 10:00 and has been a popular offering. 385-2645.

42. For poetry lovers, Davis-Kidd has **Poetry Night** the second Thursday of every month at 7:30 P.M. in the Second Story Cafe (385-2645). Local poets come to read and there is an open mike. The Barnes & Noble bookstore in Franklin at the Mallory Corners shopping center at CoolSprings also has poetry reading nights once a month. It is not at a regular time so call the store for information. 377-9979. Books-A-Million, 1789 North Gallatin Road, at Rivergate, has Poets in the Round from 7:00 to 9:00 P.M. on Fridays. 860-3133. Bookstar, 4301 Harding Road, has an open mike poetry night, Featuring You, on the first Wednesday of every month. For young children, there's a story hour at 10:00 A.M.

each Tuesday, and a theme party, like Berenstain Bears, monthly. 292-7895.

43. Media Play, with three stores: Rivergate (851-1586), **Hickory Hollow** (731-4345), **and 100 Oaks** (383-5114) has many programs for adults and children. Pick up a current flyer in the store to see what's going on.

■ *Ms. Cheap's Quick-Saving Tip:*

Check out used-book stores.

44. The Mall at Green Hills has its Kids' Club every Saturday morning at 11:00 in the East Court near Garfield's restaurant. Geared for children two to twelve years old, it features everything from magicians to storytellers to educational programs to jugglers. The "club" usually lasts about forty-five minutes. On the first Saturday of each month, it is followed by some sort of arts and crafts activity. The mall also has other family-oriented activities and events, so call 298-5478, extension 20, to get an updated bimonthly calendar.

45. Take the little ones to Bellevue Center to play at Rooland, a giant gameboard play area in the center court at the mall. Designed for children two to six years old, it's a nice break from shopping at the mall. It is also a lifesaver when you need a good rainy day outing for the little ones. It is open the same hours that the mall is open and is a self-supervised play area. In other words, don't just drop your children off and go shop. You must stay with them. 646-8690.

46. Bellevue Center mall also has free jazz music in the food court every Monday night from 7:00 to 8:30. 646-8690.

47. Enjoy the Vanderbilt University Fine Arts Gallery, Twenty-third Avenue at West End Avenue, in the old university gymnasium. This gallery has five exhibitions a year consisting mostly of thematic selections from the Vanderbilt Art Collection. Open Monday through Saturday from 1:00 to 4:00 P.M. and on Sundays from 1:00 to 5:00 P.M. Closed weekends during the summer. 322-0605.

48. Vanderbilt's Sarratt Gallery in the Sarratt Student Center also has exhibits on a regular basis. Other art possibilities at Vanderbilt are the John F. Kennedy Center (322-8240) and the Margaret Cuninggim Women's Center (322-4843).

49. Enjoy the Van Vechten Gallery at Fisk University at the corner of Jackson Street and D. B. Todd Boulevard. This gallery includes one hundred works of art from the Alfred Stieglitz collection, including works by Picasso, Cézanne, Renoir, and O'Keefe, as well as changing exhibits. Admission is free but they encourage contributions. This is one of the largest and best collections of art in the Southeast. Fisk has two other galleries, the Aaron Douglas Gallery, on the third floor of the university library, which is open from 11:00 A.M. to 1:00 P.M., Tuesday through Friday, and the Appleton Room in Jubilee Hall, which is open 10:00 A.M. to 4:00 P.M., Monday through Friday. The Appleton Room is the permanent home of the portrait of the Jubilee Singers, as well as the home of a collection of faculty works dating back to 1936. 329-8720.

50. Tennessee State University's Hiram Van Gordon Gallery has a series of exhibits throughout the year. Gallery hours are 8:30 A.M. to 4:30 P.M., Monday through Friday. The gallery is in Jane Elliott Hall (the Women's Building) on the main TSU campus, 3500 John Merritt Boulevard. 963-7509.

51. Check out the local (for sale) art galleries: Local Color, 1912 Broadway, 321-3141 (open Monday through Saturday, from 10:00 A.M. to 5:00 P.M.); **the Arts Company**, 215 Fifth Avenue North, 254-2040. Gallery hours are 10:00 A.M. to 5:30 P.M. Monday through Saturday, and one Sunday a month. **Cumberland Gallery,** 4107 Hillsboro Circle, open Tuesday through Saturday, from 10:00 A.M. to 5:00 P.M., 297-0296; **the Tennessee Art League Gallery,** 3011 Poston Avenue, (open Tuesday through Sunday from noon to 4:00 P.M.), 298-4072; **the Tennessee Artist in the Mall at Green Hills,** 254-0881 (open from 10:00 A.M. to 6:00 P.M., Monday through Saturday); **Zeitgeist Gallery in Cummins Station,** 209 Tenth Avenue South, featuring contemporary art (open from 10:00 A.M. to 5:00 P.M., Monday through Friday, and from noon to 3:00 P.M. Saturday), 256-4805; and **In The Gallery,** 624 A Jefferson Street, 255-0705 (open Tuesday through Thursday, from noon to 5:30 P.M., and on Friday and Saturday from noon to 5:00 P.M., 255-0705. They are all free. Call 781-0890 for information about special Sunday Art Matinees available at some galleries.

52. Browse the Eighth Avenue antique district. Stop first at the Downtown Antique Mall, 612 Eighth Avenue South, and then at Estelle's Consignment Furniture and Antiques, across the street at 601 Eighth Avenue South. From there, proceed to Virginia Parker's Antique Jewelry, 1016 Eighth Avenue South, and Pia's Antique Gallery, 1800 Eighth Avenue South. You'll find a cluster just past the intersection of Eighth Avenue and Wedgewood in the Douglas Corner area (the 2000 and 2100 blocks), including Antique Merchants, Cane-Ery Antique Mall, the Art Deco Shoppe, and Ejvind's Consignment.

If you backtrack to the Wedgewood intersection and turn onto Wedgewood, you'll find two more by going under the interstate: On the left is the Tennessee Antique Mall and on the right is the Wedgewood Station Antique Mall. I'm not saying that these shops and malls are cheap, just that they make for interesting browsing. And, of course, it doesn't cost a penny to look. Other quality antique malls include White Way at 1200 Villa Place in the Edgehill area, Decades on Second Avenue downtown, Belmont Antiques at 3112 Belmont Boulevard, and the Goodlettsville Antique Mall in Goodlettsville.

53. If you are a newcomer (not a tourist) why not become a volunteer? This is a great way to get involved, meet people, and help your community. A good place to start is Hands on Nashville, which is an organization that pairs volunteers with projects in all segments of the community. Walk dogs at the Nashville Humane Association, help build houses with Habitat for Humanity, help clean up bad areas, work with seniors, feed children dinner through Kids Cafe, work with Second Harvest Food Bank, etc. Just call Hands on Nashville (298-1108), go through a short orientation, and then sign up for what you are interested in.

54. Walk the trails at Radnor Lake, a state natural area. The lake was created by the L&N Railroad in 1914 to provide water for their steam engines. It then became a wildlife sanctuary in 1923. This one-thousand-plus-acre park offers six miles of hiking trails, including a great, almost flat two-and-a-half-mile trail around the lake. This is not a recreation park, but a preserve where you can see all kinds of wildlife and hundreds of species of wildflowers, mosses, fungi, ferns, and other plants. Located at 1160 Otter Creek Road, the park is open from 7:00 A.M. until sunset. Check out the free programs offered there, such as the free canoe float, children's night hikes, wildflower hikes, insect programs, and even what they call the "owl prowl." These are all free but most require reservations, so call 377-1281.

55. Visit the Warner Park Nature Center at 7311 Highway 100. The schedule here is chock-full of free stuff: nature hikes, children's activities, adult wildflower walks, owl watches, etc. Just call for information, keeping in mind there is something going on for all ages almost every day. Activities include the annual Fall Family Campfire at Percy Warner Park one Friday night in October. Bring marshmallows and a blanket, and enjoy storytelling and other activities. Or check out the star parties at the Model Airplane Field in Warner Park, where you can look through telescopes at all things celestial. 352-6299.

56. Take a trip to see the Narrows historic area of the Harpeth River. This is a nice short walk (about twenty minutes from the parking lot) and a beautiful place from which to look at the Harpeth River or have a picnic. You can see the amazing one-hundred-yard tunnel that was handcut through the rock: It is considered a major engineering feat. The Narrows is off Highway 70 in the Harpeth Scenic River Complex, about twelve miles from Charlotte Pike and Highway 70. 797-9052.

57. Enjoy a simple walk in the park. Metro has eighty-three parks, with 9,340 acres that are all yours. You should know that Nashville has more park land per capita than any other major city in the United States. Percy Warner Park, the city's largest park, is roughly three times as large as New York's

■ *Ms. Cheap's Quick-Saving Tip:*

Pick a way to exercise that is cheap or free, such as tennis, walking, skating, bike riding, etc.—activities that don't require hugely expensive equipment or country club memberships.

Central Park. The parks system also has a lot more to offer. So keep reading. 862-8400.

58. A free dip will cool you off. Metro Parks has ten pools around town (mostly inner city) that are free all summer. They include Hadley Park, E. S. Rose Park, and the Looby and Cleveland pools (regulation-size, twenty-five-yard pools); four indoor pools: at Whites Creek High School, Pearl-Cohn High School, Glencliff High School, and Napier Park; and three smaller pools at East Park, Coleman Park, and Richland Park. 862-8400.

59. Play tennis. Nashville has 160 free courts, many of which are lighted. There also is a free tennis program at Hadley Park Tennis Center. The courts at the Metro Sportsplex are the only ones that charge a fee. 862-8400.

60. Try Shakespeare in the Park in August. Every weekend in August, Metro Parks sponsors a full-length, outdoor Shakespearean performance. It is free and has received rave reviews in recent years. 862-8400.

61. There are free movies in Centennial Park. Every Tuesday in June, Metro Parks features outdoor movies. They are free and perfect for the whole family. Films recently shown have included *The Wizard of Oz, 2001: A Space Odyssey,* and *Viva Las Vegas.* Bring a blanket and/or lawn chairs and a full picnic basket, and be ready to settle back and relax. 862-8400.

62. Enjoy the Metro Parks Jazz on the Porch series in the summer, featuring jazz bands at the Two Rivers Mansion on Sundays. 3130 McGavock Pike. 862-8400.

63. In June and July there are free **big band dances at Centennial Park** on Saturday nights in the Arts Center Courtyard. 862-8400.

64. Every Thursday in May there is a **concert in the Parthenon,** meaning you get into the Parthenon free, too. 862-8400.

65. There's a full series of Parthenon Symposia lectures. Call the Parthenon for times or a full schedule. 862-8431.

66. Sign up for free ballet, tap, guitar, drum, drama, and art lessons through Metro Parks. Metro Parks offers a full schedule of free lessons for children and adults, including a set of lessons geared toward seniors. 862-8400.

The Parthenon. (Nashville Convention and Visitors Bureau)

67. Take the Centennial Park Tree Trail. There is a booklet that you can pick up at the Parthenon, and then take the (approximately) two-hour walk in the park. 862-8400.

68. Enjoy the crafts fairs that come to town, mainly in the spring and fall. TACA (Tennessee Artists and Craftsmen Association) has two wonderful annual fairs with demonstrations, craft sales, live music, and food at Centennial Park. Other big

■ *Ms. Cheap's Quick-Saving Tip:*

Go hiking.

fairs at Centennial include the annual fall Celebration (at the arts center at the back of the park), the American Artisan fair in June, and others. Check weekly listings on Friday and Sunday in the *Tennessean* to see what's coming up. The *Nashville Scene* also has listings. 862-8400.

69. The Nashville Symphony has four or five free summer concerts in various Metro Parks. Just call Metro Parks in early summer for the schedule. 862-8400.

70. Feed the ducks at Centennial Park. There are plenty of ducks at Lake Watauga, and they are usually hungry. So save that stale bread and have at it. 862-8400.

71. Take advantage of all of the festivals. These include Oktoberfest in Germantown (in October, of course), Jazzfest in Franklin in the summer, Dog Days at Elmington Park in September, the African Street Festival at Tennessee State University in September, Uncle Dave Macon Days in Murfreesboro in July, and the Murfreesboro Street Festival in May. Take the children and yourself to the Southern Festival of Books in October, for storytelling, reading, and meeting children's authors. The festival, put on by the Tennessee Humanities Council, is held on the War Memorial Plaza downtown. "Unless you are a snob, most of the festivals would be great fun," says Terry

Clements, director of tourism for the Convention and Visitors Bureau. "It's great free entertainment." Call 259-4747 for a calendar.

72. Friday nights at Track 14 at the Union Station Hotel. Jazz bands perform free on Friday nights in the late summer and during the fall months from 5:00 to 9:00 P.M. on the railroad concourse overlooking the landmark train shed. Admission is free and there's complimentary parking in the train shed. 259-3928.

73. The Fourth of July fireworks at Riverfront Park seem to get better and better every year, with recent years featuring almost thirty minutes of pyrotechnics. Parking can be a problem, but there is plenty of room in the Metro Courthouse parking lot for standing around and looking. Some people bring chairs and blankets for extra comfort. 862-8400.

74. Watch the airplanes land and take off. On a pretty day take a picnic to the runway observation area at the end of Vultee Boulevard off Briley Parkway at Textron and watch the jets take off and land. Kids love this. There are even picnic tables here. This area is officially called the Automobile Observation Area and is open from 6:00 A.M. until 11:45 P.M. 275-1675.

75. Get on the mailing list for Belmont University School of Music concerts. There are some fabulous musical opportunities here, with most of the concerts free and open to the public. The Belmont Camerata Musicale, along with the faculty concert series, provides regular free entertainment. One particular treat is the annual Camerata Christmas Concert in the Belmont Mansion. The mansion usually charges admission so this is the occasion to actually get two freebies in one: a look at the mansion and great music. For more information, call the Music Events Line at 460-5636.

NASHVILLE CELEBRITY INSIDER'S TIP

Porter Wagoner: "The Grand Ole Opry is the biggest bargain. If you go on any given Friday or Saturday night, you can see a minimum of twenty stars for under $20. And most of these stars, when they go on the road, you would pay more than that to see just them. You see people like Garth [Brooks] who are usually sold out. That is a real bargain.

"Another great thing is the Opryland Hotel. It costs you nothing to just

(Continued on next page)

76. The Blair School of Music also has a full schedule of free concerts. The Blair Concert Series is not free, but the school sponsors as many as one hundred concerts a year that are free. There are some twenty faculty concerts as well as guest concerts and student concerts that are free and open to the public. 322-7658.

77. Vanderbilt University has three public concerts a year by the Vanderbilt Concert Choir and Chamber Singers: spring, fall, and Christmas. 322-6097.

78. Tennessee State University also has grand opportunities for hearing good music. An example is the free Christmas concert featuring the university choir and Meistersingers in December. Also watch for the dates of the spring Cultural Affairs series at Tennessee State University. The series brings storytellers, actors, and singers on campus for free performances. 963-5341.

79. Fisk University, the oldest historically black college in the country (founded in 1866), also **has great music for the**

community. One of the highlights of the year occurs every October 6. That's when the university celebrates Jubilee Day with a special convocation concert by the famous Fisk Jubilee Singers. Other musical opportunities are scattered throughout the year. 329-8717.

80. David Lipscomb University has a full calendar of art and music events open to the public. The music includes concerts by the University Jazz Band, the University Concert Series, A Capella Singers concerts, and the Early Music Consort concerts. For information, call the department of music at 269-1000, extension 2258. Lipscomb also has a nice gallery, the John C. Hutcheson Art Gallery, featuring student and faculty exhibits. It's open from 8:00 A.M. to 4:30 P.M., Monday through Friday. Call 269-1000, extension 2398, for gallery information.

81. Tour historic Franklin. Okay, Franklin isn't quite Nashville, but it's real close by. Its pre–Civil War downtown square is full of specialty shops and restaurants. On the side

go in and see an unbelievable sight, with all the plants, the laser show, the Cascades, the new Delta. I've had people say, 'Porter, it was the most spectacular thing I have ever seen.' And these are people who have been to Mount Rushmore and all over the world. It takes a day to see it all."

Porter says the best food bargain he could think of was the breakfast bar at Shoney's. "It is a great buy."

streets you can find plenty of antique stores. It won't be free if you are in a buying mood, but it is a wonderful place to browse and see a beautiful historic downtown square that has been preserved and creatively redeveloped. Franklin's entire original downtown, including the Main Street shopping district, is listed on the National Register of Historic Places.

82. Dancin' in the District. This might be the best deal of all. Every Thursday from early May through late August there is a free concert at Riverfront Park featuring the likes of Emmylou Harris, Jars of Clay, Webb Wilder, and the Iguanas. This draws quite a crowd, with the average attendance running at about ten thousand for each performance. It starts at 6:00 P.M. and usually runs until about 9:00 P.M. For information, call TomKats at 256-9596.

83. Check out live music at Nashville-area coffee houses. Start with Henry's Great Coffee House, 318 Broadway; Provence Breads and Cafe, 1705 Twenty-first Avenue South; Owl's Nest, 205 Twenty-second Avenue North; Radio Cafe (262-1766), 1313 Woodland Street; and Bongo Java (385-5282), 2007 Belmont Boulevard. The music is free most of the time, but call first to check.

84. The piano music in the grand lobby of the Hermitage Hotel at the corner of Sixth and Union downtown is a great way to relax after a long day. It's also a great place to meet and chat with a friend. The piano music can be heard every day from 5:00 to 8:00 P.M. and there is no cover charge. The lovely, high-ceilinged lobby has been restored and is elegant and comfortable. The Hermitage, which opened originally in 1910, has had an impressive guest list. Six presidents and such celebrities as Bette Davis, Greta Garbo, and Al Capone have stayed here. The late Dinah Shore made her professional singing debut at the Hermitage, which at one time was also the headquarters of the women's suffrage movement in Tennessee. 244-3121.

85. The Owl's Nest Coffeehouse (205 22nd Avenue North) has a free percussion workshop the first and third Saturday of each month at 1:00 P.M. for children three through eight. It lasts about an hour and participation from the whole family is encouraged. There's no need for reservations—just show up and enjoy. 321-2771.

86. The Bluebird Cafe at 4104 Hillsboro Road is one of Nashville's premier music spots and has some great free deals. The early show at 6:30 is free every night. The cover doesn't kick in until the late show. Sunday nights are writers' nights (8:00 P.M.) and are free. Mondays at 6:00 P.M. are open-mike nights. In addition, the club holds monthly free-milk-and-cookies concerts for children as well as a free monthly seniors program. 383-1461.

■ *Ms. Cheap's Quick-Saving Tip:*

Don't buy food or drink in a movie theater. Eat before or after the show if at all possible. That way, you can get more and better food for less than you would in a theater, for sure. And you won't have to stand in those excruciatingly slow concession lines.

87. Go to Christ Church on Old Hickory Boulevard to hear the Christ Church choir. Services are at 8:30 and 11:15 A.M. The huge choir, accompanied by a full complement of musicians, has made five recordings and toured several times. The church claims a membership of five thousand members, including a number of stars such as the Judds. 834-6171.

88. Go to Tootsie's Orchid Lounge at 422 Broadway, a landmark on Broadway. There is free music here all day and night, starting at 10:00 A.M. with a single entertainer and then moving into three shifts of bands that play until 2:00 A.M. Tootsie's close proximity to the Grand Ole Opry house made it famous, with its original owner, the late Tootsie Bess, being a friend to up-and-coming stars in need. 726-0463.

89. Go to Robert's Western Room at 416 Broadway. There is music from 9:00 A.M. until 2:00 A.M. and no cover. The band changes every four or five hours. The store sells cowboy boots and hats along with T-bone steaks, burgers, and the like. 256-7937.

90. Check out Mulligan's Pub and Restaurant at 117 Second Avenue North. This Irish establishment has live entertainment, Thursday through Saturday starting at 9:30 P.M., and there's no cover. It's usually Irish music, but once a month classic rock 'n' roll is offered. There is also sometimes a solo entertainer on Wednesday nights. 242-8010.

91. Enjoy free music every night with no cover at Wolfy's at 425 Broadway. It's everything from rockabilly to a forties swing band. Music starts at 9:00 P.M. and there is very rarely, almost never, a cover. 251-1621.

92. Don't miss the Midnight Jamboree at Ernest Tubb Record Shop, 2414 Music Valley Drive. This one is for the night owls, starting at midnight every Saturday of the year. It's a live country music show broadcast from the

Texas Troubadour Theater over WSM radio. It features Opry stars as well as up-and-comers. Doors open at 11:30 P.M. The show is from midnight to 1:00 A.M. 889-2474.

93. Visit the Hindu Cultural Center of Tennessee, at 521 Old Hickory Boulevard. The Hindu temple, which opened in 1991 in the Bellevue area, is recognized as one of the most beautiful Hindu temples in North America. The temple provides religious services and a place for cultural events for the one thousand midstate families who are members of the Hindu community. 356-7207.

94. West Nashville Founders Home and Museum is a replica of James and Charlotte Robertson's 1779 double log cabin, located in H. G. Hill Park, behind the West Police Station at 6730 Charlotte Avenue. Free, but not open regular hours. 297-1551.

95. Nashville's Patio Party at WSM-TV (5700 Knob Road) offers an all-you-can-eat break-fast that is provided by Loveless Cafe and, get this, it's *free*. So is the hour and a half of live entertainment. Arrive at the station by 5:15 A.M. during the summer months to get seated. Door prizes awarded! No need to call ahead.

■ *Ms. Cheap's Quick-Saving Tip:*

Make friends with other cheap people. Cheap people need to stick together and share information on deals.

96. Enjoy free music at the Station Inn's jam sessions. The bluegrass club is located at 402 Twelfth Avenue South and almost always has a Sunday-night, no-cover-charge jam session. 255-3307.

97. Pick up the *Nashville Scene,* which is Nashville's leading alternative newspaper. It's free, it comes out every Wednesday, and it's full of information about what's going on around town, with club listings, movies, and chatter. It's available in many groceries, clubs, stores, etc.

98. Take a walk up and down Second Avenue and just browse and people watch. This street has it all: eclectic shops, lots of street activity, a Nashville flavor, and big-time entertainment. And you don't have to spend a dime, unless you want to.

99. Take a ride to the top in one of the glassed-in elevators at the Holiday Inn Crowne Plaza. The hotel, which was Nashville's first high-rise hotel, is at 623 Union Street, and the elevators are a big hit with the kids. 259-2000.

100. Take advantage of the free fishing day every June. It's always on a Saturday and you can fish free with no license anywhere in the state. The Tennessee Wildlife Resources Agency usually has a special kids-oriented fishing event with drawings and other activities. 781-6622.

101. Tour the Downtown Presbyterian Church, 154 Fifth Avenue North, with its Egyptian Revival Architecture. This church was designed by William Strickland and is on the National Register of Historic Places. During the summer months the front doors are open and tour guides conduct formal tours. In the winter you can enter through the church during office hours (8:00 A.M. to 4:00 P.M.) and ask for a tour. Construction of the church began in 1849, and it was dedicated on Easter Sunday in 1851. The church now has 175 members. 254-7584.

More Freebies

Okay, let's not stop at 101. Here is more free stuff to do, although just a few miles away:

• Attend the Leanna Opry in Leanna, Tennessee, about thirty minutes from Nashville between Smyrna and Murfreesboro. The Opry, which is put on by Sophie Tipton and Louise Tinberlay, has been described as "Tennessee at its purest." It starts at 6:00 P.M. and is free, although they do pass the hat to pay the bands—so it's a free activity with an asterisk. The show is held in the old Bethel schoolhouse on the second and fourth Saturdays of each month, October through March. They sell hamburgers, hot dogs, etc. and for dessert, homemade banana pudding. 896-0623 or 896-2458.

• If you like the Leanna Opry, you might also want to try the Almaville Opry the third Saturday night of each month, October through March. It's mostly bluegrass, with some gospel and country. It's free and there is a concession stand with homemade chili, burgers, and homemade pies. It starts at 6:00 P.M. Take I-24 from Nashville to exit 70 and turn right on Almaville Road. Go six miles into the Almaville Road community and there you will find the Opry in the Almaville school house. Bertie Mae Maxwell is the organizer. 893-4732.

• Take a trip to Tennessee wine country. I suggest

"Any night of the week you can find free entertainment," says Butch Spyridon, executive director of the Convention and Visitors Bureau. Among his suggestions:

For adults:
Tootsie's Orchid Lounge
Robert's Western World
Gerst Haus on Saturdays
Tapings at the Wildhorse or TNN
Wolfy's
Opryland Hotel lounges

Opryland Hotel. (Donnie Beauchamp photo, courtesy of Nashville Convention and Visitors Bureau)

Other hotel lounges
Station Inn on Sundays for the bluegrass jam session
Universities' concert series

For children:
Malls
Ben West Library, also other libraries
Metro Parks
Bookstores

nearby Clarksville where you can tour the Beachaven Vineyards and Winery. There are free monthly jazz concerts in the summer. It is open from 10:00 A.M. until dark, Monday through Friday, and noon to dark on Sunday. You even get to sample some of the fine wine products. (931) 645-8867.

• Tour the Jack Daniel Distillery in Lynchburg. This is the nation's oldest registered distillery. There are guided tours every day from 8:00 A.M. to 4:00 P.M., except for Thanksgiving, Christmas, and New Year's Day. Visitors get to see the whole process of making sour mash whiskey, including Jack Daniel's charcoal mellowing process that has been used for more than a century. The tour lasts between seventy and ninety minutes. Directions from Nashville: Take I-24 east toward Chattanooga and get off at exit 111. Turn left onto Highway 55 through Manchester and Tullahoma into Lynchburg. (931) 759-6180.

• You can also tour the George A. Dickel Distilling Co., on Cascade Hollow Road in Tullahoma. There are guided tours, Monday through Friday, from 9:00 A.M. until 3:00 P.M., except holidays. The tour takes at least forty-five minutes. (931) 857-3124.

• Drive the Natchez Trace. It starts off Highway 100 near the Loveless Motel north of Franklin. In the fall the Tennessee Department of Tourist Development has a fall foliage hot line (1-800-697-4200) to inform where the best colors are.

• Cannonsburgh Pioneer Village in Murfreesboro, at 312 Front Street, is a living history museum of southern life. It includes a log house, blacksmith shop, general store, grist mill, one-room schoolhouse, church, and museum. It is open, May through October, Tuesdays through Saturdays, from 10:00 A.M. to 5:00 P.M., and from 1:00 to 5:00 P.M. on Sundays. (615) 893-6565.

• Middle Tennessee State University has a lot of good stuff going on, particularly in art and music. Check out Art Barn Gallery, which is open 8:00 A.M. until 4:30 P.M., Monday through Friday, when the university is open. (615) 898-5653.

• For great music on the MTSU campus in Murfreesboro, check the Middle Tennessee Symphony, the Middle Tennessee Choral Society, and the MTSU Concert Choir performances throughout the year. Call (615) 893-6527 for information. There is also a schedule of concerts by the Stones River Chamber Players. (615) 898-2476.

• There is a bluegrass jam session one night a month from 7:00 to 10:00 P.M. in the Assembly Hall at Cedars of Lebanon State Park. (615) 443-2769.

• How about a Cajun outing? All you need to do is take an hour's trip to Milton, Tennessee, and visit Manuel's Cajun Country Store on Friday or Saturday night. The Cajun music, starting at 6:00 and going until 9:00, is set up outside the store and is free to all who want to listen. Inside, Cajun dinners are served (not necessarily cheap, at $6 to $12 per dinner). To get to Manuel's, take I-24 to Murfreesboro to the Highway 96 East exit. Milton is between Lascassas and Auburntown. The trip should take about fifty minutes from Nashville. This may be a little-out-of-the-way place, but owner Abe Manuel says on a busy night he draws a crowd of about six or seven hundred people. (615) 273-2312.

Moneysaving Deals

These are not free, but they are deals you should know about.

• Spend a Tuesday at the Cumberland Science Museum, 800 Fort Negley Boulevard. Admission is half-price on Tuesdays. Regular price is $6 for adults and $4.50 for children, ages three through twelve. A family of four visiting on a Tuesday could save a lot. 862-5160.

• The Country Music Hall of Fame, 4 Music Square East, is a great place for country music fans to visit. The only discounts I could find were $1 off with a coupon from the chamber of commerce coupon book and $1 off for AAA members. The $10 tour has three components: (1) a look through the museum, (2) a tour of Studio B, and (3) a trolley tour of Music Row. Also, locals should know that if you pay full admission once, you should sign up for the Ambassador Program, which gives you either free or half-price admission on any subsequent visit if you bring someone with you. 256-1639.

• Check out the area lakes for a family swim. They are not free but are quite cheap. Old Hickory Lake and Percy Priest Lake between them have nine different cheap beaches, complete with white sand (well, almost white), restrooms, roped-off swimming areas, picnic tables, and even playgrounds in some cases. They all charge $3 per car or $1 per person to get in. There is no charge for children twelve and under. Some have an attendant, while others have an honor box for your admission money.

Old Hickory's six offerings include: Old Hickory Beach at the dam on the Old Hickory side; Laguardo in Wilson County on Highway 109; Cedar Creek Beach in Mount Juliet; Lock 3 Beach in Hendersonville; Avondale in Hendersonville; and Lone Branch in Wilson County near

Laguardo. Call 822-4846 for more info or directions to these beaches.

The three J. Percy Priest Lake beaches are: the beach at the end of Anderson Road, which is the biggest; and the beaches at Seven Points Recreation Area and Cook Recreation Area, both in the New Hope Road/Stewarts Ferry Pike vicinity. For information on the Percy Priest swimming, call 889-1975.

• Go fishing. In addition to the big lakes, there are some other less-imposing options, at Lake Watauga in Centennial Park, at Willow Pond on Highway 100 in Warner Park, and at the lake at Shelby Park. Fishing licenses are required for children over twelve. Licenses cost $2.50 for a day license or $21 for a year. They are sold in hunting and fishing stores.

• Enjoy a picnic at literally hundreds of fabulous places. Nashville is blessed with a variety of scenic picnic spots: Riverfront Park, with the Cumberland River traffic floating by; Centennial Park, with the fabulous Parthenon as the setting; young-children-oriented parks such as Fannie Mae Dees Park near Vanderbilt; Estes Park just off Woodmont; Drakes Creek in Hendersonville; beautiful creekside sites in Percy Warner Park; riverside and lakeside sites at Shelby Park; and playground picnic areas at Cedar Hill Park. Picnickers have their pick. Some of them can be reserved. 862-8400.

• Go to the Wave Country pool after 4:00 P.M. and get in for half-price. Operated by Metro Parks, this pool is at Briley and Two Rivers Parkways. It has the added advantage of not being so crowded, especially if you have little ones. Wave Country, by the way, allows you to bring a picnic. The pool is open between Memorial Day and Labor Day, seven days a week.

• Ride the trolley downtown. You can actually get a tour if you just board and ask the driver for information. It's less than a dollar.

• Visit the Parthenon in Centennial Park, at West End and Twenty-fifth Avenues. The Parthenon, which was created for Nashville's centennial celebration in 1897, is the world's only reproduction of the Greek Parthenon. Be sure to see Athena, the largest indoor sculpture in the western world, created by Alan LeQuire, as well as the city's art museum. Admission is $2.50 for adults and $1.25 for seniors and children ages four through seventeen, and there are even coupons to make it cheaper. Children under four are admitted free of charge. 862-8431.

• Plan on the mini-*Nutcracker*. Every year in early December, the Metro Parks ballet program puts on a wonderful

Ten perfect places to have a picnic:

• **Riverfront Park**

• **Centennial Park**

• **Percy Warner Park**

• **Edwin Warner Park**

• **Steeplechase Field**

• **Two Rivers Park**

• **Shelby Park**

• **Opryland**

• **Drakes Creek in Hendersonville**

• **Automobile observation area at the airport**

• **(Radnor Lake is not for picnicking. They won't let you eat there.)**

abbreviated version of *The Nutcracker*. It is very professionally done and perfect for young audiences. Call Metro Parks for dates and admission prices, which are very reasonable. 862-8400.

• Mark your calendar for the Tennessee State Fair in September and take the whole family for less than $10 (if you make the most of the coupons and special deals.) The ten-day run includes a circus, pig races, a close look at all kinds of animals, a cultural exhibit, and lots of fun. 862-8980.

• Make a trip to the Belle Meade Plantation during the annual Fall Fest, the third weekend in September. You can get in for $2 instead of the usual $7. 356-0501.

■ *Ms. Cheap's Quick-Saving Tip:*

Watch movies on network or basic cable television. If you wait long enough, the movie you've long wanted to see will make it right into the convenience of your home, and even without benefit of a premium cable channel.

• Sounds baseball games are cheap. Tickets start at $3 each. To get the price down even further, watch for some of the many promotions and deals. 242-4371.

• Take advantage of discount movies at Cinema North 6 near Rivergate (859-0639) and at the Old Hickory Cinemas 16

Belle Meade Plantation. (Robin Hood photo, courtesy of Nashville Convention and Visitors Bureau)

(865-7992) in Madison. These seats can be as cheap as 50¢ or $1 a person, depending on when you go.

• Attend Vanderbilt women's basketball games and contests in other sports at Vanderbilt—lacrosse, tennis, soccer, baseball. Ticket prices are very reasonable. For example, season tickets to Vanderbilt women's basketball games this last season were $78 for adults (only about $5 a game) and $25 for youth (less than $2 a game). For schedules and ticket information, call 322-GOLD. Check out other local university schedules as well.

• Catch a flick at the Sarratt Cinema on the Vanderbilt campus. There is a great schedule and seats are always $3. Or buy a Sarratt Nashville Film Society Any 10 ticket for $25. These ten passes can be used for any screening. 322-2424.

• Ice skating at the Metro Sportsplex can be lots of fun. It is open day and night. For public skating times, call 862-8480.

• The Nashville Zoo and Nashville Wildlife Park at Grassmere have lots of promotions—such as buy-one-get-one-free deals throughout the year. Call for a schedule or to ask about special deals. The Nashville Zoo is located in Cheatham County. Take I-24 west to exit 31, and then take a left on New Hope Road and follow the signs (370-3333). The National Wildlife Park at Grassmere is in south Nashville, at 3777 Nolensville Road (833-1534).

• **Travellers Rest,** the 1799 historic house museum, has a cheap day one day a year: April 9, the birthday of its builder, John Overton. Overton was a legal and political advisor to Andrew Jackson, and he served as a judge in the Tennessee Supreme Court. The house, which has a regular adult admission of $6, is open Tuesday through Saturday, from 10:00 A.M. to 5:00 P.M., and on Sunday from noon to 5:00 P.M. It is at 636 Farrell Parkway off Franklin Road. 832-8197.

• One of the best values around, if you are a *real* country music fan, is to go to Fan Fair. A ticket costs $90 and gives you admission to a week's worth of entertainment, a chance to meet and greet the stars, and even an opportunity to have your picture taken with them. Every year there are more than one hundred stars participating and usually more than thirty hours of great music scattered throughout the week. If you want to go, plan ahead because they sell out early. The first reservations are taken in November for the June event. That's a lot of entertainment for $90. 889-7503.

MS. CHEAP'S
"Top Ten"
Ways to Save at Least $100 This Year

There are a lot of ways to save money—a little here and a little there. And the little-by-little approach can add up to substantial savings. Here are my favorite ways to save a little—and, ultimately, a lot.

1. **Brown bag your lunch** a couple days a week if you work outside the home. You not only save money but can also save time. If you add up $5 a day for lunch, it can become big bucks.

2. **Instead of buying a replacement wardrobe each season, buy one really nice multiseason outfit** that can be mixed and matched with what you already have. You fellows might buy a couple of great ties instead of springing for a new suit. You can still look good without a major purchase.

3. **Couponing on groceries and other things** is one of my favorite ways to save. It can be very effective. In my family of four, I average $8 to $10 a week in savings by using coupons.

4. **When you eat out, order water instead of soft drinks.** You'd be surprised at how that keeps the cost down.

5. **Watch for and act on specials for items you use a lot,** whether they be toilet paper, cola, beer, green beans, or whatever. The stock-up-and-save ads make a lot of sense.

6. Shop around for major purchases. There can be a world of difference in the price of everything from a leaf rake to a summer vacation. Call around, look at ads.

7. Turn down the heat. A difference of a degree or two is money.

8. Try to find one outfit for each family member at a thrift or consignment store. It might take several trips but you could get hooked on this kind of "never know what you will find" kind of shopping. I have found all kinds of great things for myself, our daughters, and even for my husband.

9. Have a yard sale to get rid of things you are not using. This, too, is a life-enriching experience as well as a way to create more room on the budget for other things. We've found that it is a lot more fun if you have a goal for the proceeds of the sale, such as deciding before the sale to use the money for a vacation or for new clothes for the upcoming season.

10. Pay bills on time. This includes paying off your credit cards each month and keeping the card issuers from tacking on unnecessary interest. Also, pay your utility bills before the due date to avoid the penalty charges. There can be a big difference.

■ *Ms. Cheap's Quick-Saving Tip:*

A reader once told me, "Use it up, wear it out, make it do, or do without!"

f o u r

Nashville, Featuring the District

So, What's the District? you ask. It's the only happening place in downtown Nashville. It is one place you must visit if you want to experience all of Nashville. The geographic area is just up from the Cumberland River and takes in Second Avenue, Printers Alley, and Lower Broadway. These days it is very eclectic, with historic turn-of-the-century warehouse buildings, funky shops, interesting boutiques, clubs, restaurants, street vendors, and hip new places to browse.

MS. CHEAP'S
"Top Ten"
Tips on How to Save on the Top Ten Attractions in Nashville

Just because an attraction is on the top-ten list doesn't mean it has to cost top dollar. There are all kinds of discounts, deals, and even free things out there. I asked the folks at the Nashville Area Chamber of Commerce to help me identify ten of the top attractions in Nashville, so that I could list them and show you where you could save. Note: Some of the material presented in this list also appears elsewhere in this book, but I bring it all together here in one convenient spot for the visitor or consumer who has a week or less to hit as many high points as possible in and around Nashville.

Add it up, and save up!!

1. **The Grand Ole Opry.** This is already pretty reasonable at $18.00 plus tax per ticket for the nighttime performances, which present twenty-five performers or so. Of course, you could always watch portions of the show on TNN, or just listen to it on WSM radio as people have been doing since 1925. 889-6600.

2. **Nashville Zoo.** The zoo is a big promoter, with all kinds of buy-one-get-one-free deals, free days with certain driver's licenses, etc. Call to find out what promotions exist and look for dollar-off coupons in booklets such as the chamber of commerce's visitor coupon book. 370-3333.

3. **The Tennessee State Museum.** A freebie! 741-2692.

4. **The Parthenon.** This museum houses the Athena statue as well as a wonderful art collection and costs only $2.50 per adult, so it is a bargain already. Look, too, for coupons in places such as the *Entertainment Book* and the chamber's book.

5. **Country Music Hall of Fame.** There is a dollar-off coupon in the chamber discount book, and if you sign up to be an ambassador you get a discount on any return visits, provided you bring somebody with you.

6. **The Hermitage.** Andrew Jackson's fabulous home has one free day during the year and also an occasional dollar-off discount in places such as the chamber book.

7. **The Wildhorse Saloon.** Go early and save. It's free before 5:00 P.M. every day. There's no cover charge if you get there before 5:00 P.M. Then stay as long as you like—for free!

■ *Ms. Cheap's Quick-Saving Tip:*

Walk when you can, instead of driving.

8. **Ryman Auditorium.** This one offers almost no discounts but you can at least go into the gift shop.

9. **Belle Meade Plantation.** There are dollar-off deals from time to time, but no big specials.

10. **The Tennessee Foxtrot Carousel,** which was scheduled to open in the summer of 1998 at Riverfront Park, is all about art and fun. It is expected to become one of the top attractions in Nashville. Created by Nashville native Red Grooms, it features interesting

Country Music Hall of Fame. (Nashville Convention and Visitors Bureau)

faces and places of Tennessee—such as Davy
Crockett, Roy Acuff, Kitty Wells, Wilma Rudolph, and
more. At press time, the exact cost to ride the carousel
was not set, but it was expected to be in the $1 to
$1.50 range.

Cheap Days

A gift from Music City to you—three really cheap days in Nashville! Sounds too good to be true? Well, I'm here to tell you it can be done. And there is still more to do, when you get finished with these three days.

Cheap Day One: Downtown

Total cost: Free except for parking, lunch, and dinner.

1. Start with a visit to the free Museum of Tobacco Art and History at the corner of Eighth Avenue North and Harrison Street.

2. Then walk over and spend the morning looking at the Bicentennial Mall and touring the state capitol.

3. Have lunch at Farmers Market, where there are five fun and very moderate restaurants, or the Arcade (count on $4–$6 per person). The Arcade is a collection of restaurants and shops in a historic arcade setting.

Wildhorse Saloon. (Donnie Beauchamp photo, courtesy of Nashville Convention and Visitors Bureau)

4. The afternoon could be spent walking the Nashville Citywalk (a self-guided walking tour), touring Fort Nashborough, and browsing through the Tennessee State Museum.

5. Have an early dinner at a moderately priced place such as San Antonio Taco Company, the Old Spaghetti Factory, or even the Hard Rock Cafe, and make it to the Wildhorse Saloon in time to get in free for a taping before 7:00 P.M.

6. If you are still wanting music when the taping is over, check out Wolfy's, Tootsie's, or Robert's Western Room—all on Broadway, all with music, and all with no cover charge.

Cheap Day Two: The Opryland Hotel area
Total cost: Free, except for parking, lunch, and dinner.

1. Start the day with the free Grand Ole Opry Museum.

2. Shift over to the hotel for lunch in the Delta food court (about $5–$6 per person) and a postlunch walk around the Delta, Conservatory, and Cascades.

3. Take a break and walk or ride the trolley shuttle over to the Factory Stores of America outlet mall across the street.

4. There are moderately priced restaurants on Music Valley Drive, such as Shoney's, Cock of the Walk, Santa Fe,

and the restaurant in the Ramada Inn. The cheapest restaurant in the Opryland Hotel (other than the food court) is Rachel's Kitchen, where you can expect to pay anywhere from $6–$10 per person.

5. After dinner, trek back to the hotel to take in the free Cascades water-and-light show featuring pianist Vince Cardell, and then enjoy the music in the hotel's various lounges.

6. If this is Saturday, you should wander back across the street to the Ernest Tubb Record Shop and Troubadour Theater for the Midnight Jamboree.

This is a full day.

Cheap Day Three: Gallery Day, along with some antique browsing

Total cost: Free, except for the modest Parthenon admission and meals.

1. Nashville is blessed with art galleries and you could easily spend an entire day engrossed in them. For example, you could spend the morning at the Van Vechten Gallery at Fisk University, shift over to the Vanderbilt Fine Arts Gallery on West End Avenue, and then swing in to Centennial Park to see the Parthenon and its galleries.

2. How about a picnic lunch on the grounds at the Parthenon? A convenient food choice would be Hog Heaven, a little eating place just behind McDonald's on the west side of Centennial Park. It's known for its barbecue and for its vegetables. Several other prominent yet moderately priced eating establishments are an easy walk, such as Mosko's on Elliston Place.

3. More art is available at local galleries such as Local Color, Cumberland, and Zeitgeist—if you still want it.

4. Late-afternoon activities could include a big browse along the Eighth Avenue antique district.

5. If you still have shopping to do, go out Eighth Avenue to Thompson Lane and try the stores in the 100 Oaks Mall. A good place to eat near there is the Calypso Cafe on Thompson Lane, just across the street from the mall.

6. Check out the free music early at the Bluebird Cafe, or check the listings in the papers to see about writers' nights or other entertainment with no cover charge.

Parking in Downtown Nashville
The first, and perhaps most challenging part of "doing downtown" is parking. The cost for parking can run anywhere from free–$15 a day, so it pays to shop around. The average parking for a day is $4–$6. Alright Parking has sixteen locations and Central Parking has fifteen, so there really is plenty of space available. The challenge is to find it without paying big bucks.

Free Parking: You can manage this if you find a place at a parking meter at night (after 6:00 P.M.) or on the weekend after noon on Saturday. The other free parking is in the state parking lots behind the state capitol and on the north side of James Robertson Parkway.

Cheaper parking: Most of the cheap parking is on the south side of Broadway in the area beyond the new arena. Other more centrally located good bets are the Metro Riverfront parking lot, which is 50¢ an hour; a Central Parking garage on Seventh between Church and Commerce, which at one point had $1 parking after 3:00 P.M.; and the Criminal Justice Center garage just north of the Metro Courthouse, which is $3.75 for the day; or the Church Street Centre Garage which is $4 all day.

Most expensive: The Metro Courthouse parking lot, which tops out at $18.25 for eight hours, and the First American Center's garage, which is $15 all day.

Now that you've parked, it's time to explore.

Nashville's skyline at dusk. (David Wright photo, courtesy of Nashville Convention and Visitors Bureau)

What do you need to browse? Start with:

1. good walking shoes,

2. a couple of hours,

3. a Downtown Discount Card, which you can get from the chamber of commerce's Downtown Partnership and which has all kinds of discounts for things in the District—such as 10 percent off in shops, free cover charges, and free dessert or appetizer with entrées in certain restaurants (to get this card, call 259-4763), and

4. a sense of adventure.

What's on Second?

Second Avenue is full of browsing opportunities, good restaurants, music, and people-watching, particularly in the summer months when the sidewalks are dotted with street vendors doing everything from Tarot fortune-telling to shoe shines to hot dog sales.

Here are some of the favorite stops on Second:

• The Wildhorse Saloon dance club, at 120 Second Avenue North, is a place you must stop in at night. This is an experience that is sooooo Nashville. If you get there before 5:00 P.M., they will waive the cover. They have line dance lessons from 4:00 to 9:00 P.M. every day during peak season.

• Take a walk down Butler's Run, 138 Second Avenue North, where you will find an assortment of shops, such as Cinemonde, which shows and sells movie posters and other collectibles; and Southwest and Beyond, which is a very nice shop with cards, jewelry, candles, and posters—all with a southwestern flair.

• Check out You're the Star recording studio at 172 Second Avenue North, where you can make an audio or video tape as if you were a real professional. This is not cheap, but if you use a coupon from your Downtown Discount Card, it helps. Regular prices are $24.95 for a video tape or $16.95 for the audio.

• Laser Quest, 166 Second Avenue North, is a neat place to go if you're in the mood for games. It is not too expensive, and the Downtown Discount Card gives you a break. 256-2560.

• The Gothic Shop, 166 Second Avenue North, is an interesting store, featuring all kinds of gargoyles, wall pieces, landscaping pieces, sconces, pedestals, etc. It's fun to look.

• Land of Odds, 174 Second Avenue North, is a fun shop, with incense, unique postcards, beads, Christmas ornaments, and cool jewelry. You could spend some time in here.

• Decades, at 110 Second Avenue North, is one of my favorite places to browse. It is a memorabilia gallery with everything from old gas pumps and signs to magazine covers and poster art. The store has several stores within it, including a Fudge Factory with a soda fountain downstairs; Hot Dogs and Cool Cats, a petlovers' shop; a record shop; and a Christmas Shop.

• Visit the Market Street Emporium, 112 Second Avenue North, where you will find Baskin-Robbins, Chicago Lunch,

Just Java coffee shop, a tattoo shop, the Second Avenue Smoke Shop, and a handful of other unique ventures.

• Other shopping opportunities on Second are the Hard Rock Gift Shop and the Wildhorse Gift Shop in the Wildhorse Saloon. As you might guess, these are not cheap, but hey, it's fun to look.

• You could take a self-guided tour at the Market Street Brewery and Public House, 134 Second Avenue North. See how handcrafted beer is made by the Bohannon Brewing Company. There is no official tour, but

■ *Ms. Cheap's*
Quick-Saving Tip:

Stop buying things you don't

need or really want.

the restaurant is glassed so that you can see the process. The restaurant staff is glad to answer questions if you have any. It's open the same hours as the restaurant, 11:00 A.M. to midnight. 242-8223.

• On the other side of the street, check out the glittery Dangerous Threads, 105 Second Avenue North, where the stars shop; Market Street Mercantile, at 111 Second Avenue North; and Crazy Man T's, 113 Second Avenue North, where T-shirts are the main business.

• On the same side, check out Mulligan's Pub, at 117 Second Avenue North. This Irish pub-restaurant has live entertainment every Thursday through Saturday starting at

9:30 P.M. and no cover. It's usually Irish music but once a month there's classic rock 'n' roll. There is also sometimes a solo entertainer on Wednesday nights. 242-8010.

On Broadway

Broadway, like Second, is a mixture of old and new, and of entertainment, food, and shopping. The north side has more to offer than the south, but check out both.

• Visit Hatch Showprint at 316 Broadway, which has been in business since 1879. This is an antique letterpress working poster company that designs and prints contemporary entertainment posters as well as select reproductions from the 117-year-old collection. It is fun to come in and look at the posters Hatch has produced over the years for events ranging from sports to vaudeville to current star concerts and album cover designs. It is open, Monday through Saturday, from 10:00 A.M. to 5:30 P.M. Call about Sunday hours. 256-2887 or 256-2805.

• Another step back in time is Acme Farm Supply at 101 Broadway. This is an old-fashioned feed and seed store with everything you need for your garden or your pet. It is more touristy than it used to be, but the feed and seed part is by far the most interesting. 255-5641.

NASHVILLE CELEBRITY INSIDER'S TIP

Country Music Star Jo Dee Messina: "I love to shop at Wal-Mart (Hermitage) because I can always get what I want at a reasonable price. Satco (San Antonio Taco Company) has great food. It's quick, easy, and inexpensive."

- Stop in the two record stores on the south side of Broadway—Lawrence Brothers (256-9240) and the world-famous Ernest Tubb Record Shop (255-7503), which was the original home of the Midnight Jamboree. These are fun places to browse.

- Tomkats Hot Stuff, at 408 Broadway, is a small shop featuring "eclectic gifts," marinades, and other goodies. It's big on hot sauces, with two hundred types to choose from. The store is one piece of a bigger entertainment complex that will ultimately include a showcase club and restaurant in the 408 Broadway building. 256-9596.

- Gruhn Guitars, at 400 Broadway, is a specialty guitar shop that is more than twenty-five years old. It is worth a stop if for nothing else than to just browse and dream. Owner George Gruhn is nationally known as a guitar dealer and has many unusual pieces for sale. And if you want to know anything about guitars, it's not hard to engage the very knowledgeable owner in conversation. 256-2033.

- Enjoy free music every night with no cover at Wolfy's at 425 Broadway. It has everything from rockabilly to a forties swing band. Music starts at 9:00 P.M. and there is very rarely a cover. 251-1621.

- Go to Tootsie's Orchid Lounge at 422 Broadway. This is a piece of Nashville history and gives you a chance to hear some free music, night or day. The late Tootsie Bess befriended many a struggling musician behind the bar of this original Grand Ole Opry-area honky-tonk. It's lots of fun, with no cover and extra-cold beer. 726-0463.

• Go to Robert's Western Room at 416 Broadway. There is music from 9:00 A.M. until 2:00 A.M. and no cover. The band changes every four or five hours. 256-7937.

• Cotton-Eyed Joe, at the corner of Broadway and Second, is a full-fledged Nashville souvenir shop with T-shirts, postcards, western wear, etc. 726-3302.

• Check out the pawn shops; there are several down there.

Eating on Second and Broadway

You have to eat while you are doing the District, and there are lots of economical choices:

• San Antonio Grill, 208 Commerce. You can easily eat here for under $5 and enjoy some really good Mexican food. The soft chicken tacos and the chips and salsa are always good. There are even a few tables outside. Go to a counter, order, and take your food to the table. That way, tips are not part of the equation. 259-4413.

• Hard Rock Cafe, 100 Broadway. Hard Rock has been very successful in the District and is not outrageously priced. You can eat for under $7 for lunch or dinner. One of the best little-known deals is the Friday breakfast buffet, where there is a live radio broadcast, good food, and an interestingly mixed crowd of entertainment and downtown business people. Breakfast was less than $5 the last time we checked. 742-9900.

• Demos Steak and Spaghetti House, 300 Commerce. This restaurant gets great reviews at lunch and dinner and usually has a hefty line at lunch time. There is a daily lunch special that is always a good deal. Dinner is pricier but not outrageous. 256-4655.

• Merchants Restaurant, 401 Broadway. Great lunch specials are in the $3.99–$5.99 range. Again, dinner can be expensive. 254-1892.

• Wolfy's, 425 Broadway. Good sandwiches and daily specials at lunch. 251-1621.

• Riverfront Park. Get a sandwich and have a picnic while watching the Cumberland River traffic. There are lots of places to sit.

• Jack's Barbecue, 416 Broadway. This is just what you'd expect—good Nashville barbecue. If the weather is cooperative, eat out on the patio in the back or take it to go for your picnic at Riverfront Park. 254-5715.

■ *Ms. Cheap's Quick-Saving Tip:*

Help your children and/or grandchildren learn to save money. One way to do this is by matching what they spent with what they could have spent, or otherwise encouraging them.

• BellSouth Cafeteria in the BellSouth Building at 323 Commerce Street. A very inexpensive spot for breakfast or lunch. This would also be a good place to grab a sandwich for a Riverfront Park picnic. It's open until about 1:30 P.M. on weekdays. 742-0261.

• Carolyn's Homestyle Kitchen, 330 Charlotte. This features homestyle vegetables, fried chicken, etc., on the north end of the District almost to the courthouse. It's open for weekday lunches only. 255-1008.

• Old Spaghetti Factory, 160 Second Avenue North. This is a good bet for lunch or dinner, with pasta, salad, bread, etc., all for one very inexpensive price. This is probably the best deal on the street for dinner. 254-9010.

• Mère Bulles, 152 Second Avenue North. Burgers, salads, and other choices are very affordable on the lunch menu. 256-1946.

• Market Street Brewery and Pub, 134 Second Avenue North. Good burgers, sandwiches, salads, and of course the Market Street beers. 259-9611.

• The Diner—Not operating at press time, but it is expected to be a fun diner/malt shop once it opens just south of Broadway.

• Chicago Lunch, in Market Street Emporium at 112 Second Avenue North. The menu includes hot dogs and the like. 726-3171.

• Baskin-Robbins, in Market Street Emporium at 112 Second Avenue North. It has that good ole ice cream everybody loves. 256-4670.

• Laurell's 2nd Avenue Oyster Bar, 123 Second Avenue North. This is a great place for soup, if you are looking for good and affordable. The seafood is great but sort of pricey. 244-1230.

• Big River Grille, 111 Broadway. Good for sandwiches, soups, and salads. 251-4677.

• Fast Food—I hate to eat fast food when I'm on vacation, especially when there are some interesting local restaurants for about the same price. No matter, if you are looking for fast value food, there is a Wendy's at 113 Second Avenue North, Sbarro at the corner of Second and Commerce, a Dairy Queen at 212 Fourth Avenue North, and a Schlotzsky's at 220 Second Avenue North.

Beyond Second Avenue

Second Avenue and Lower Broadway are where the action is, but there are other hot spots and points of interest within just a few blocks:

• Walk along the Cumberland River or just sit and relax in Riverfront Park. Get an ice cream cone or a sandwich from somewhere on Second and sit and watch the river traffic, or even see a boat being launched from across the river.

• Take the Nashville Citywalk. This is a great way to see Nashville. Designed by the Metro Historical Commission, it's self-guided and includes historical as well as entertainment stops. The complete walk is about two miles, winding past just about everything you need to see downtown. You can start at Fort Nashborough or just follow the dotted blue line from whatever point you land on it. To get a brochure about the Citywalk, stop by the visitors center in the new arena at Fourth and Broadway.

• Tour Fort Nashborough. The fort, which is a replica of the original fort that defended Nashville in the 1780s, is interesting to walk through. Situated along the river on First Avenue just north of Broadway, it is open from 8:30 A.M. until 4:30 P.M., Monday through Saturday, and is free.

• Walk through or have lunch in the Arcade, a turn-of-the-century mall that runs from Fourth to Fifth Avenue between Church and Union. Built as a replica of an arcade in Italy, Nashville's Arcade now houses very modestly priced lunchtime restaurants and a few shops. 255-1034.

• Walk up to Fourth Avenue and tour the Ryman Auditorium, which is as much a museum as it is a rejuvenated performance venue. Admission is $6 for adults and $2.50 for children to tour this former home of the Grand Ole Opry but it's worth it to see if you are an avid country music fan—and especially if you believe that you might catch a glimpse of Hank Williams's ghost there. The Ryman has a nice gift shop, and you can get in there without paying the admission price. Hours for self-guided tours are 8:30 A.M. to 4:30 P.M. daily.

If You Need Basics

I love Second Avenue and the District but it is not the place to shop for basics. Just climb up the hill to Fifth and Church and you'll find most everything you might need in the way of film, a toothbrush, headache medicine, deodorant, emergency underwear, or whatever.

I call Fifth Avenue "Practical Street." Locals who work or frequent downtown know that Fifth between Church and Union Streets is the place to shop for basics. There is a full-sized Walgreen's drugstore, as well as a Family Dollar Store.

The Trolley

Nashville's trolley service is very reasonable and fun. The best bargain is the three-day pass which sells for $5.00 and provides unlimited riding for three days on the trolley. Otherwise, it is $1 per ride for most routes. Get a pass at the Visitors Center at the Nashville Arena.

Country Music Star Mark O'Connor: "The Taqueria on Nolensville Road is one of my favorite places to eat Mexican food. It's great food for little money."

Think about trying out these creative ways to use the trolley:

• If you are "doing" Music Row and the District, park free in the Music Row area and ride the trolley to Second Avenue. This has the added advantage of avoiding the hassle of parking and driving downtown. This is an option during the summer season when the trolley runs every thirteen minutes.

• Park free in the Bicentennial Mall area north of the capitol and take the parking shuttle up to downtown proper for 30¢. This is a weekday deal.

• Use the trolley as a tour. One Ms. Cheap reader suggested this one. She says if you sit up front and ask a lot of questions of the driver, you can get as good a tour of downtown as the paid official tours. MTA spokesman David Warren says the drivers are trained to give a spiel but admitted that "some are better than others."

• Take advantage of the trolley in the Opryland Hotel area. During the peak season, it runs between the Opryland Hotel, the Factory Stores of America outlet mall, and all along Music Valley Drive.

For information on schedules and routes, call MTA customer service at 862-5969.

f i v e

Consignment Shopping

Consignment shopping has come into its own in Nashville over the last few years. There are more than twenty clothing shops in the immediate area and, boy, do they have deals. There are also a half-dozen or more furniture and household goods consignment shops that have what you need at a fraction of the cost of new pieces.

One of the most refreshing things about consignment shops is that these are small businesses, which usually means the owner is there in person, working with and welcoming customers. These owners often know their customers by name and are genuinely interested in helping them. They take pride in their shops and, in most cases, have done a good job of merchandising.

Almost all of the clothing shops specialize in women's or children's clothes, but a handful carry men's as well. Although the furniture shops vary in terms of the percentage the consignor and the shop get (anywhere from one-third to a sixty-forty to a fifty-fifty split). Most of the clothing shops work the same way. People bring in their clothes, and the consignment store sells them. The proceeds are usually split fifty-fifty between the consignor and the store.

Consigning is really a pretty simple proposition. Somebody brings merchandise in to sell; somebody else buys it; one makes money; one saves money. It's recycling at its best.

Before listing and describing the shops, I'll go over a few general hints for shoppers and consignors.

MS. CHEAP'S
"Top Ten"
Tips for Consignment Shopping

1. **Shop often.** The inventory changes daily as consignors bring new things in, so stopping by every several weeks or even more often can pay off.

2. **Tell the shop owner or manager what you want or need.** These are small business owners and most are willing to watch out for you. Most of the shops have a wish list where you write down what you want and they will call you if they get it.

3. **Call the shop before you go.** Although most of them have established hours, some are flexible. One owner said she was always open unless her children were sick. Another one had a sign on the door saying that she was closed because she was away for two weeks for her wedding.

4. **Know your brand names and what things cost new** before you go. This gives you a better idea of how much you are really saving.

5. **Find out when things go on final clearance sale.** Here's when you will find the rock bottom prices.

6. **If you want to be a consignor, visit the shops first to see** which one seems most suited to what you are going to sell.

7. **Be sure that your things are pressed, clean, and spotless** because most of the shops are pretty particular. It is embarrassing when they tell you your things are not up to standard.

8. **Call the shop you want to deal with before you go.** Some require an appointment or have special criteria for the proper delivery of clothes.

9. **Be sure you know the store's policy on things that are left** before you leave your things. Many of the shops donate to charity the things you don't pick up, but you should know that before you get involved.

10. **Be sure to find out how and when they pay—** whether you have to come by to get a check or whether they will send it.

Clothing consignment stores you might like to try out:

• Bargain Boutique, 4004 Hillsboro Road in Green Hills Court. In business for more than twenty-five years, this is Nashville's oldest consignment store. Owner Kay Alexander started it as a fling and now has 400 to 500 consignors at any given time. The store features women's clothes for every occasion. It is all clothes—no shoes or accessories. The store is very boutiquish, with friendly and helpful sales people. One unique aspect about Bargain Boutique is that the merchandise is marked with the name of the person who is selling it, meaning that if you are lucky enough to find a consignor with your size and taste, you can follow her wardrobe. Alexander has a customer from Birmingham, Alabama, who sends her clothes to the store, and a woman from San Antonio, Texas, who likes the Birmingham woman's clothes. "She asks us to call her when the Birmingham woman is mailing and then she and her husband drive down in a van." Open 10:00 A.M. to 5:00 P.M., Monday through Saturday. 297-7900.

• Classique Boutique, 2541 Park Drive, off Lebanon Road in Donelson. Owner Linda Kitchens has been open for several years and features mostly women's but some men's and children's clothes, as well as shoes, accessories, after-five, and wedding dresses. Kitchens has 475 consignors. Open Monday through Saturday, 10:00 A.M. to 6:00 P.M. 872-8891.

• The Closet Club, 265 White Bridge Road. Open since early 1996, this shop is all ladies' clothes, shoes, accessories, after-five, and bridal. Owner Donna Forsythe has a sale room where most items are $3 and $5. Open Tuesday through Saturday, noon to 6:00 P.M. 353-8604.

• The Clotheshorse, 5133 Harding Road, in the Belle Meade Galleria. Owned by Linda Summerville, this is all women's items, with designer labels, formal wear, wedding dresses, hats, jewelry, and shoes. In business for over five years, the store has 1,500 consignors. (In the same center, there are two or three other stores you should check out—Bodacious Books, a great used book store, and the Clearing House, which is a furniture consignment store. There is also a vintage clothing store that sells some items on consignment.) Hours are 10:00 A.M. to 6:00 P.M., Monday through Friday, and 10:00 A.M. to 5:00 P.M. on Saturday. 352-2804.

• Consignment Shop, in Alexander Plaza in Franklin. Owner Frances Byrd has been in business for more than a decade, selling ladies' clothes, accessories, shoes, and after-five wear. She has more than 4,000 consignors. Open 9:30 A.M. to 5:00 P.M., Monday through Saturday. 794-5980.

• Consigning Women, 5604 Nolensville Road, in the Wal-Mart Center at Old Hickory Boulevard. The motto here is "Dress like a celebrity on a 9–5 budget." This store, which has been open for several years, doubled its space in 1996 and has 2,000 consignors. It carries men's and women's clothes. This nicely organized shop has shoes, accessories, plus sizes, and after-five. Owners Shirley Shrader and Mary Sims are almost always there. Open 10:00 A.M. to 6:00 P.M., Monday through Saturday. 832-7026.

• Designer Renaissance, in Green Hills behind Kinko's on Hillsboro Road. Owned by Jodi Miller, this popular out-of-the-way store (you almost have to know where it is, so a call might not hurt) has three rooms full of great consignment merchandise that comes from 1,500 consignors. It's everything from casual to after-five and wedding and also includes shoes, belts, and lots of jewelry. Open 10:00 A.M. to 6:00 P.M., Monday through Saturday. 297-8822.

• Designer Resale, 613 B West Main Street, Hendersonville, has been in business since 1992 selling ladies' designer clothes. Owner Sue Brame has 300 consignors

■ Ms. Cheap's Quick-Saving Tip:

Shop around on any purchase you make—large or small. Do *not* buy the first thing you see.

and offers a very good selection of formal wear, wedding wear, sportswear, shoes, bags, and accessories. Open Tuesday through Friday, 10:00 A.M. to 6:00 P.M.; and Saturday, 10:00 A.M. to 5:00 P.M. 822-8881.

• Fashion Connection, 5115 Nolensville Road in Tusculum Square, and a newer store at 4735 Old Hickory Boulevard. The store carries women's, men's, and juniors', as well as shoes, accessories, and after-five. The motto is "Look like a million without spending one." The shop is divided into specialty shops—the Men's Shop, Trend Tent for juniors, Top of the Shop for designer wear, and the Plus Shop for bigger sizes. Open Monday through Thursday, 10:00 A.M. to 8:00 P.M.; Friday and Saturday, 10:00 A.M. to 5:00 P.M. Ask about the 250 Club that offers special deals. 333-2632.

• Judy's Friends, 914 B Woodland Street. Owner Judy Armstrong has about 500 consignors. It is mostly women's with a few "Sunday dresses" for girls, all designer. Open 10:00 A.M. to 6:00 P.M., Tuesday through Friday; 10:00 A.M. to 5:00 P.M. on Saturday. 262-3061.

• Jelly Beans, at First and Main in Franklin. This shop, opened in 1995, is children's and maternity, with merchandise in sizes running from 0 to 14 in girls and 0 to 4 in boys. It also carries baby equipment and furniture. Open Tuesday through Saturday, from 10:00 A.M. to 5:00 P.M. 591-6886.

• Just Kidding, a children's consignment boutique in the Belle Meade Galleria, 5133 Harding Road. Owner Mary Harrington has clothing, shoes, furniture, toys, books, etc. for newborns up to preteens. Consignors are asked to call for appointments for the reviewing and pricing of items. Proceeds split 50-50. Open Tuesday through Friday, 10:00 A.M. to 6:00 P.M.; Saturday, 10:00 A.M. to 5:00 P.M. 356-3991.

• Just Kids Stuff, 7028 Church Street East, in Brentwood Station near Wilson Pike Circle. This store is just what it says—for kids only. But it has all kinds of stuff—clothes, cribs, strollers, car seats, toys, etc. Drawing from a pool of 425 consignors, the selection is good, with some new merchandise mixed in with the slightly used. Open 9:00 A.M. to 5:30 P.M., Monday through Friday; 9:00 A.M. to 5:00 P.M. on Saturday. 221-9849.

• Kangaroo's Pouch Consignment Shop, on Highway 96 in Franklin in Alexander Plaza. It has more than 700 active consignors and sells everything for babies and children up to pre-teen. Also a big selection of maternity. Open 9:30 A.M. to 5:00 P.M., Monday through Friday; 10:00 A.M. to 5:00 P.M. on Saturday. 790-7800.

• Mother's Favorite, 5532 Nolensville Road. Located in the Wal-Mart Center (same center with Consigning Women), this established store is owned by Deborah Bridges and has close to 4,000 consignors. It has infants through size 16 in girls and 20 in boys and also carries maternity clothes, baby furniture and accessories, shoes, bedding, and other items. Open Monday through Thursday 10:00 A.M. to 7:00 P.M.; Saturday, 10:00 A.M. to 8:00 P.M.; and Sunday, 1:00 to 5:00 P.M. 834-7767.

• Passarounds, 121 Stadium Drive in Hendersonville. Just off Gallatin Road, this shop for women, children, and infants, is chock-full of good things from more than 900 consignors. It also has maternity fashions. In business since the late 1980s, it is currently owned by Lisa Majors, who also carries baby equipment and furniture. Caters to working moms and stay-at-home moms; no after-five. Open 10:00 A.M. to 5:00 P.M., Tuesday through Saturday. 822-9065.

■ *Ms. Cheap's Quick-Saving Tip:*

Make consignment shopping a priority. There are lots of savings to be had here, especially in ladies' and children's clothing.

Consignment furniture is another way to save big.

• Play It Again M'aM, 158 Belle Forest Circle in Bellevue. This shop, which has been open since 1994, features designer women's clothes and accessories, as well as household goods. Owner Merrylane Barnes has more than 600 consignors. Open Tuesday through Friday, 10:00 A.M. to 6:00 P.M.; Saturday, 10:00 A.M. to 4:00 P.M. 646-7910.

• Second Impressions, 416 Main Street in Franklin. Owner Jean Hall has been in business since 1991 and has 1,500 consignors. She carries designer clothing, shoes, accessories, and some after-five. Hours are 10:00 A.M. to 5:00 P.M., Monday through Saturday. 790-3477.

• Second Time Around, 235 East Main Street, Hendersonville (in the Kmart Shopping Center). Peggy

Armstrong's shop is laid out like a boutique and manned by helpful sales clerks. Shoppers are even offered a soft drink as they browse. While the merchandise is not all designer, it is in good shape. "We are real picky," Armstrong says. The store draws from 400 consignors and has a strong showing of after-five and bridal, as well as a good shoe selection. Open 10:00 A.M. to 5:00 P.M., Tuesday, Wednesday, and Friday; 10:00 A.M. to 7:00 P.M., Thursday; and 10:00 A.M. to 4:00 P.M. on Saturday. Closed Sunday. 822-6961.

• Yellow Brick Road, 4722 Old Hickory Boulevard in the Hermitage Crossings Shopping Center. Owned by Deborah Swartwood, this shop opened in 1994 and caters to children and mothers-to-be. With 300 consignors, the store carries clothes from infants to size 16 for boys and girls. It also carries maternity wear and baby furniture, accessories, toys, costumes, ballet items, and equipment for babies. Open Monday through Friday, 10:00 A.M. to 5:00 P.M.; Saturday, noon to 5:00 P.M. 871-9009.

• Young Generation, 992 Davidson Drive in West Nashville. This well-organized store has been in business since 1980. Owned by Carol Calvert, it features children's and women's clothing, accessories, and toys and equipment for babies and young children. Also books, tapes, Nintendo, videos, etc. The store has a rack of greeting cards for 50¢ each. Open 10:00 A.M. to 5:30 P.M., Monday through Friday; 11:00 A.M. to 4:00 P.M. on Saturday. 352-7803.

Furniture consignment stores

Here it is clearly in your best interest as a consignor to call and find out all kinds of information, such as:
• What will they take?
• What's the percentage split?

NASHVILLE CELEBRITY

INSIDER'S TIP

Grand Ole Opry Star Jan Howard says: "I shop end-of-season sales at the better shops. I love to find something that I admired at full price and then see it on sale at somewhere like Grace's or Gus Mayer. I've gotten great jackets at two-thirds off. Sometimes I tell them to call me when they mark it down another third. And sometimes they will do it right there. That happened just the other day.

(Continued on next page)

• Will they pick your things up?

• Will they help you unload if you bring things to them?

• Are there items they just don't take?

• How much will they price your items for?

• How long will they keep them if they don't sell?

• How do they pay you (e.g., monthly)?

• Do they mail your payment or do you have to pick it up)?

Now for a list of Nashville furniture consignment shops:

• The Clearing House in Belle Meade Galleria, on Harding Road, offers a mix of $1,000-plus antiques right down to $3 items. There are rugs, crystal, lamps, silver, art, mirrors, couches, chairs, lamps, etc. The Clearing House, with roots stretching back more than twenty-five years, is open three months at a time, so it is a good idea to call to get a schedule. There are no markdowns until the final week of each three-month sale. At that time, if you want something they have left, the prices are really great. Open Tuesday through Saturday. 352-9451.

• Estelle's Consignment Furniture and Antiques, 601 Eighth Avenue South. This store is just south of downtown, next door to Arnold's restaurant and across the street from the Downtown Antique Mall. The front half is consignment and the back is more like an antique mall setting. Very interesting merchandise. Open 10:00 A.M. to 6:00 P.M., Monday through Friday; 1:00 to 6:00 P.M. on Sunday. 259-2630.

• Finders Keepers has two locations, the six-thousand-square-foot store at 5125 Nolensville Road (333-9801) and a fifteen-thousand-square-foot

"Also, a lot of people don't know that if you buy something at full price and they mark it down, within thirty days, they will give you the sale price. I had that happen with a $300 dress that I bought and then saw it marked down to $150 when I went back a couple of weeks later. They gave it [the difference] to me. "I love a bargain."

store in Bellevue at the corner of Old Hickory Boulevard and Highway 70 (646-3444). They sell everything from show samples to antiques, as well as rugs, art, crystal, china, and

knickknacks. They are big on service, being the only shop in town that will come to your home to see the pieces and take them to the store at no charge. Owner Darryl Overton has been in business for five and a half years. Sofas that would have originally sold for $800 are about $350, while a dining room suite that would have sold for $2,000–$3,000 sell for under $1,000 in the consignment setting. Open 10:00 A.M. through 6:00 P.M., Monday through Saturday. Closed Sunday.

■ *Ms. Cheap's Quick-Saving Tip:*

Be prepared to negotiate a price, or get the store to throw something in for free. If you are buying something that has to be delivered, see if they will waive the delivery charge. If you are buying a washing machine, ask if they have any free detergent. Ask and ye may receive.

• Hollywood Boutique, an eclectic goods store, 451 Bell Road in Charlton Square at the corner of Bell Road and Old Hickory Boulevard. There is some furniture but more merchandise like records, pictures, comics, and glassware, and all very economically priced. Owner Karen Hollywood will even trade. She has posted a sign that says, "If you want to trade some of your cool stuff for my cool stuff, let's talk." Open 11:00 A.M. to 8:00 P.M., Monday through Thursday; noon to 8:00 P.M., Friday through Sunday. 399-0652.

• Ivy Crest Gallery, 1501 Franklin Road. This store on Franklin Road south of Concord Road, has lots of great furniture and accessories. This is a good bet. Open 10:00 A.M. to 5:00 P.M., Tuesday through Saturday. 377-0676.

• The Pink House in Berry Hill, at 2833 Bransford Avenue, is small but always fun to visit. The little house is full of good antiques and other used goodies. Open 10:00 A.M. to 6:00 P.M., Monday through Saturday; 1:00 to 5:00 P.M. on Sunday. 292-2195.

• The Rivergate Consignment Gallery, on Gallatin Road just north of Rivergate Mall. This place is huge and has furniture, antiques, rugs, pictures, etc. The merchandise turns quickly, so people shop here often. It's been open since 1993. Open 10:00 A.M. through 6:00 P.M., Monday through Saturday; 1:00 to 6:00 P.M. on Sunday. 859-2690.

s i x

Outlets

Everybody talks about Nashville being Music City. Well, it's Outlet City, too, when you stop to think about it. There are two major outlet malls and one smaller outlet mall right here, and more to come.

• 100 Oaks, on Thompson Lane at Sidco Drive, used to be a regular mall. In fact, it was Nashville's first enclosed mall when it opened in 1967. But now, after a complete multimillion-dollar redevelopment in 1995, it is a hybrid outlet center-value center and it is truly a great place to shop.

There are forty-four stores and the mall is open from 10:00 A.M. to 9:00 P.M., Monday through Saturday; from noon to 6:00 P.M. on Sunday.

Stores include: American Cellular, Bentley Luggage, Bible Factory Outlet, Bon Worth, Burlington Coat Factory Warehouse, Casual Corner Outlet, Casual Corner Woman, Chao Praya, Claire's, Colours and Scents, Dress Barn, Electronic Express, Famous Footwear, Florsheim Factory Outlet, FootQuarters, Fragrance Outlet, Furniture to Go, General Nutrition Center, the Great American Cookie Company,

Hit or Miss, Nevada Manufacturing Jewelers, OFF 5TH Saks Fifth Avenue Outlet, the Pair Tree, Paper Factory, Petite Sophisticate, Rack Room Shoes, Reebok, Rue 21, Sbarro, Stained Glass Works, Steak and Spud, Sunglass Hut, Taco Bell, TCBY, Totally 4 Kids, Warehouse Golf, Welcome Home, Treasures, Comp USA, Luxury Linens, J.C. Penney Outlet, Media Play, Michael's, PetsMart, and T J Maxx.

The mall is owned by Belz Enterprises, a diverse developer with lots of traditional retail properties and outlets around the country. There is more to come at 100 Oaks, with a restaurant planned for an outparcel and with a major theater complex coming on the property.

BIG TIP: Stop by the mall office and ask for coupons. They usually have a coupon book with coupons averaging 10 percent at many of the stores. That's a real deal when it's already off price or otherwise discounted. 383-6002.

• The Factory Stores of America Outlet Center, on Music Valley Drive across from the Opryland Hotel, is a wonderful strip center with almost eighty stores. I've had good luck in many of them, including the Casual Corner store, the Chicago Cutlery store, the Levi's outlet, the Gap, and Reading China and More. There is plenty of parking and a mini-food-court where you can get a sandwich, ice cream, coffee, etc.

Stores include: Adidas, Big Dogs Sportswear, Boston Traders, Bugle Boy, Capacity, Capers, Duck Head, Geoffrey Beene, Izod, Jerzees, Levi's, the Logo Zone, London Fog, Spiegel, Sweatshirt Company, T-Shirts Plus, Van Heusen, Aileen, Bon Worth, Casual Corner, Norty's, Petite Sophisticate, Westport, Casual Corner Woman, Westport Woman, Casual Male, Big & Tall, Farrah, S&K Menswear, L'Eggs/Hanes/Bali, Lovable, Carter's Childrenswear, Genuine Kids, Claire's Accessories, Jewelers of Las Vegas, Pegasus Jewelers, Prestige Fragrance, Boot Factory, Factory Brand Shoes, Florsheim Shoes, Hushpuppies, Genesco Shoes, Keds/StrideRite/Sperry Topsiders, Rack Room, SAS, Pepperidge Farm, Sara Lee, Black and Decker, Carolina Linen, Country Clutter, Dan River, Famous Brand Housewares, Heritage Lace, Hoover Company, Kitchen Collection, Libbey Glass, Oneida, Oops! Art Outlet, Reading China and More, Welcome Home, Walnut Bowls/Chicago Cutlery, Bible Factory Outlet, Foozles Extraordinary Book Store, Leather Loft, Luggage Warehouse, Music 4 Less, Outlet Gifts, Paper Factory, Russ, Totes/Sunglass World, Toy Liquidators, and Wallet Works. 885-5140.

• The Music City Outlet Mall, 900 Conference Drive in Goodlettsville, just off the I-65 Long Hollow Pike exit, is small but worth a stop if you are out that way. Stores include: H.I.S. Chic Outlets, Body Blasts, Wholesale Wallpaper, Hit or Miss, Linens N Things, Dress Barn, K&E Outlet, Dollar General, Velma's Cake and Candy, Shoe Palace, and Acme Boot. 783-1000.

• Not a mall but almost as big as one is the Genesco Factory to You Shoe Store at the Genesco headquarters, 1415 Murfreesboro Road. (It is a twenty-thousand-square-foot store featuring twenty thousand pairs of men's and women's shoes as well as some men's clothing, luggage, and accessories. The store carries all of the Genesco brands (Johnston and Murphy, Dockers Footwear, Jarman, etc.) as the core, and then dozens of others, such as Rockport, Reebok, Naturalizer, Timberland, Keds, and others. It is Genesco's flagship store for sure and has probably a mix of 70 percent men's and 30 percent women's.

The store has quite a following, with cabs bringing shoppers (largely businessmen) over from the nearby airport daily. Shoes are overruns, seconds, and discontinued styles. Discounts are generally 30 to 50 percent off. Don't miss the Value Center at the back of the store, where shoes take further markdowns. That is where I start, and then work my way to the front. Genesco's Boot Factory is next door and carries Dan Post and Code West boots, among others. Both stores are open from 9:00 A.M. until 7:00 P.M., Monday through Saturday; noon to 6:00 P.M. on Sunday. Seniors (sixty-two and older) get a 10 percent discount on Wednesday. 367-7413.

■ *Ms. Cheap's*
Quick-Saving Tip:

Use store brands. Some are better than others, but in most cases my family can't tell the difference. One sure bet is Sam's Cola from the Sam's and Wal-Mart people. Our taste test found it to be indistinguishable from the "real thing."

If Nashville's three outlet malls are not enough for you, there are literally dozens more within a four-hour drive. Here are a few, with a sampling of stores listed for each destination.

1. Pigeon Forge/Sevierville

• The Tanger Factory Outlet, on Highway 441 in Pigeon Forge, is the area's most upscale outlet mall, with Anne Klein, Boston Traders, Eddie Bauer, J. Crew, Liz Claiborne, London Fog, JH Collectibles, Wembley Tie, and Eagle's Eye stores. (423) 428-7001.

• Pigeon Forge Factory Outlet Mall, on Highway 441, with Arrow, American Tourister, Boston Traders, Chicago Cutlery, Black and Decker, Mikasa, Oshkosh B'Gosh, Polly Flanders, Manhattan, Gorham, Bass Company, Jaymar, L'Eggs/Hanes/Bali. (423) 428-2828.

• Belz Factory Outlet Mall, also on 441, has Bass, Bugle Boy, Bruce Alan Bags, Cape Isle Knitters, Capezio, Casual Corner, Converse, Etienne Aigner, Famous Footwear, Fuller Brush, Maidenform, Levi's, Naturalizer, Nike, Nine West, Jonathan Logan, Jaymar, Sony, Socks Galore and More, Regal, Royal Doulton, and Van Heusen. (423) 453-7313.

• Five Oaks Factory Stores, on 441 in Sevierville, is smaller than its competitors but loaded with upscale outlets. It has Guess? Baby Guess? Adolpho II, Brooks Brothers, Dan River, Dexter Shoe, Johnston and Murphy, Lenox, Magnavox, Nautica, Norty's, Pepperidge Farm, Reed and Barton, Rockport, Socks Galore and More, Tool Warehouse, and Woolrich. (423) 453-8401.

2. Memphis

• The Belz Factory Outlet Center, just east of Memphis at Canada Road and Interstate 40, was the first outlet mall built new in the entire nation. Tenants now include Bass, Boot Factory, Bugle Boy, Casual Corner, Corning Revere, Danskin, Ducks Unlimited, Gentleman's Wearhouse, Hit or Miss, Maidenform, Linens 'N Things, Rack Room, Regal, the Ribbon Outlet, Toy Liquidators, Van Heusen, and Westport Limited. (901) 386-3180.

3. Murfreesboro
• The Outlets Limited mall on I-24 at exit 78-A features Acme Boot, Bass, Duck Head, Leslie Fay, Linens 'N Things, Hush Puppies, London Fog, Van Heusen, Dress Barn, Electronic Express, and Izod. (615) 895-4966.

■ Ms. Cheap's Quick-Saving Tip:

I love outlet malls, especially if you can find things on sale. A word of caution, though: Not everything in an outlet mall is a bargain, so know your brands and your merchandise.

4. Lebanon
• The Outlet Village of Lebanon opened in the spring of 1998 with big upscale names like the Gap, Tommy Hilfiger, Eddie Bauer, Coach, Brooks Brothers, DKNY, OshKosh B'Gosh, Jones New York, Polo Ralph Lauren, and more. This is a mall of forty-five tenants that was developed by Prime Retail, the same people who own Warehouse Row in Chattanooga. Lebanon is about thirty minutes east of Nashville on I-40 (615-444-0433). There is also a Hartmann Luggage Outlet in Lebanon at the Hartmann Factory on Baddour Parkway (449-8000).

5. Chattanooga
• Warehouse Row and Warehouse Row II, in beautifully renovated warehouse space in downtown Chattanooga, are among the most upscale outlet centers in the region. Stores include: Bass, Big Dog Company, Chico's, Cole Haan,

Colours by Alexander Julian, Danskin, Ellen Tracy, Johnston and Murphy, Geoffrey Beene, Guess?, I. B. Diffusion, Nautica, Perry Ellis, J. Crew, Ruff Hewn, Tanner, and Van Heusen. (423) 267-1111.

6. Crossville

• Factory Stores Of America has an outlet center in Crossville at the I-40 and Genesis Road interchange. It has Aileen, Bass, Bon Worth, Danskin, Fieldcrest, Cannon, Vanity Fair, L'Eggs/Hanes/Bali, Libbey Glass, London Fog, Paper Factory, Wallet Works, Welcome Home, Westport, and others. (931) 484-7165.

7. Boaz, Alabama

Boaz, like Pigeon Forge/Sevierville, is a big-time outlet destination, with four sprawling malls from which to choose. To get there, take I-59 to Gadsden, and then go north on 431 to Boaz. The centers are all on 431 or Billy Dyer Boulevard.

• Boaz Outlet Center has Athlete's Foot, Bass, Bon Worth, Burlington, Capers, Capezio, Carter's Childrenswear, Childcraft, Corning/Revere, Dress Barn, Ducks Unlimited, Everything's $1, Famous Brand Housewares, Farah, Fieldcrest Cannon, Fruit of the Loom, Hush Puppies, Izod Gant, Jaymar, Jerzees, Jockey, Jonathan Logan, Judy Bond, Leather Loft, Libbey Glass, Maidenform, Naturalizer, Oneida, Pfaltzgraff, Reading China and More, Royal Doulton, Swank, and Tie One On. (205) 593-9306.

• Factory Stores of America's Center has Adidas, American Tourister, Black and Decker, Carolina Clock and Rug, Izod Gant, Paper Factory, and Wembley Tie. (205) 593-2930.

• Fashion Outlets features Arrow, Ashleigh Morgan, Bible Outlet, Dress Barn, Duck Head, Eagle's Eye,

Etienne Aigner, Genuine Kids, Gold Toe, JH Collectibles, Johnston and Murphy, Jones New York, London Fog, Nike, Polo Ralph Lauren, Levi's, and Strasburg Lace. (205) 593-1199.

• Tanger Factory Outlet, featuring Allen Edmonds, Barbizon Lingerie, Bass, Bugle Boy, Cape Isle Knitters, Chaus, Eddie Bauer, Geoffrey Beene, Gotham, Leslie Fay, Liz Claiborne, Mikasa, Oshkosh B'Gosh, Reebok, Umbro, and Van Heusen. (205) 593-9038.

8. Kentucky

Kentucky has two options for you to consider:

• West Kentucky Factory Outlet, in Eddyville off I-24, features Aileen, Arrow, Barbizon, Black and Decker, Bon Worth, Book Warehouse, Boot Factory, Boston Traders, Brass Factory, Brown Shoe, Bugle Boy, Capers, Corning/Revere, Damon/Enro, Designer Linens by Bibb, Etienne Aigner, Florsheim, Guess?, Hush Puppies, Libbey Glass, Jonathan Logan, L'Eggs/Hanes/Bali, London Fog, Nike Sports Outlet, Reebok, Oneida, Oshkosh B'Gosh, Paper Factory, Polo Ralph Lauren, Rack Room Shoes, Walnut Bowls, Chicago Cutlery, Wembley Ties, and Westport. (502) 388-7379.

• Jent Factory Outlet, in Horse Cave off I-65, features Acme Boot and Western Wear, Aileen, Arrow, Barbizon Lingerie, Bass, Book Warehouse, Brass Factory, Bugle Boy, Capers, Casual Corner, Corning/Revere, Florsheim, Fruit of the Loom, Izod Gant, Jaymar, Kitchen Collection, Libbey Glass, London Fog, Socks Galore and More, Rack Room Shoes, Totally Ties, Toy Liquidators, Van Heusen, and Welcome Home. (502) 786-4446.

We all know malls are not everything. There are great out-of-the-way places, great destinations for scavengers and cheapos to shop. Here are a few of my faves:

1. Off Broadway Shoe Warehouse, 1501 Broadway, with savings ranging from 30 to 70 percent off on thousands of pairs of ladie's shoes. 254-6242.

2. The Shopping Bag at Bethlehem Center, 1417 Charlotte Avenue. 329-3386.

3. The Salvage Store at 119 Third Avenue South, just off Broadway. 242-8473.

4. Tabletop and Gifts, 4094 Hillsboro Road, upstairs in the Bradford Center. 292-5030.

5. Lighting for Less, 209 Tenth Avenue South on the lower level of Cummins Station. 244-3333.

6. Williams Salvage, 127 Third Avenue South. 256-6636.

7. Associated Salvage, 121 Third Avenue South. 255-2707.

8. Play It Again Sports, two stores, at Bell Forge at Hickory Hollow (731-9077) and at 7104 Crossroad Boulevard at CoolSprings (373-1097).

9. Frugal Fabrics, 3329 Murfreesboro Road. 641-2188.

10. Goodwill, with fifteen midstate stores:
- 3049 Dickerson Road. 262-0609.
- 4507 Charlotte Avenue. 297-4774.
- 1592 Fort Campbell Boulevard, Clarksville. (931) 645-2310.
- 2280 Lebanon Road. 874-2116.
- 131 South Water Street, Gallatin. 452-7886.
- 3101 Gallatin Road. 226-5546.
- 300 North Cumberland in Lebanon. 443-5105.

- 112 E. James Campbell Boulevard, Columbia. 840-0484.
- 260 West Main Street, Hendersonville. 826-0878.
- 1224 N.W. Broad, Murfreesboro. 867-9377.
- 2708 Franklin Road. 298-4866.
- 2625 Murfreesboro Road. 399-7074.
- 786 Two Mile Parkway at Rivergate. 851-6871.
- 5031 Lebanon Road, Old Hickory. 773-1659.

11. Hadassah Thrift Shop, 850 Hillsboro Boulevard. 352-1099.

12. This N That Thrift Shop, 5007 Georgia Avenue. 292-4032.

13. Salvation Army stores at:
- 140 North First Street. 259-2348.
- 2700 Nolensville Road. 259-0735.
- 6214 Charlotte Pike. 352-1154.
- 1014 Mercury Boulevard, Murfreesboro. 890-2258.
- 1135 Gallatin Road. 227-9597.

■ *Ms. Cheap's Quick-Saving Tip:*

Shop thrift stores. It's a treasure hunt, but you can find lots of great stuff and it's fun not knowing what you might find.

14. Norbert's Home Decorating Outlet, 3734 Nolensville Road, with an eclectic mix of items from popular catalog merchants, discounted 30–80 percent. 315-9800.

15. The Gold Kiser Company Store, 2823 Bransford Avenue in Berry Hill, full of used and re-usable goodies gathered from garage and estate sales, auctions, warehouse buys, dumpster dives, houses being demolished, etc. 383-3411.

s e v e n

Eating Out

Nashville dining is becoming more and more diverse in all of the price ranges. That's the good news. The better news, of course, is that Ms. Cheap goes for the lower end, where there are plenty of good options. And I don't mean fast food or cafeteria food (which, incidentally, there is plenty of, too).

Everybody knows that you can get a meal for under $3 at Taco Bell, that there are special values at places such as McDonald's and Wendy's, and that Subway, Picadilly, and Luby's offer a good value. But in Nashville there is more. What follows is a list of my favorite places where you can eat for around $6 per person. There are a few exceptions where it runs more like $7 but they are such a good value I can't resist.

In many cases, to stay under $6 requires drinking water with your meal, but hey, water is good for you. The point is these are all places where you can get good food (maybe even great food) at a good fair price. I've marked the places with this $$ sign where my $6 limit might be a stretch. In alphabetical order:

• Amerigo's, 1920 West End Avenue, for Italian lunch and dinner. Moderate price, but check out the Early Bird Special between 5:00 and 5:45 P.M., when there are five of the most popular dinners for right at $7. Otherwise, most everything is between $6.50 and $10. Open 11:00 A.M. to 10:00 P.M., Sunday through Thursday; 11:00 A.M. to 11:00 P.M., Friday; noon to 11:00 P.M. on Saturday. 320-1740. $$

• Amy's at Saint Cloud Corner, 500 Church Street, a good weekday lunch option downtown. Daily specials, sandwiches, soups, and homemade desserts. Hardly anything is over $6, with some choices as little as $3.50. Hours are 11:00 A.M. to 2:00 P.M., Monday through Friday. 242-2697.

• The Arcade, downtown between Fourth and Fifth Avenues just north of Church Street, is a beehive of activity during lunch hour, offering a food court of sorts in a historical setting. All of the eateries have most, if not all, of their menu items, within our price range. It's very diverse, with restaurants including Maney's House of Pizza, Maggie's, the Calypso Cafe, Phillip's Delicatessen, Greek Touch, Oriental Lunch, Jimbo's Hot Dogs, Las Brisas Mexican, and Grinder's Switch sandwich shop. The Arcade itself is open weekdays from 6:00 A.M. until 6:00 P.M., with most of the restaurants open from midmorning to midafternoon. Maney's, which sells pizza by the slice, as well as other things like the popular pepperoni roll and spinach roll, is the exception, staying open until 5:00 P.M. The long line at lunch every day attests to the quality and popularity of Maney's. Fortunately, the line moves quickly, as do most of the other restaurant lines.

• The Arena Food Court, in the new arena on Broadway at Fourth Avenue South. At press time these restaurants were not open on a daily basis, but there were plans to have them open to the public for lunch some time in 1998. It might be worth checking out. This would be the perfect place to gather up all the brochures from the Visitors Center and study them over lunch.

• Arnold's Country Kitchen, 605 Eighth Avenue South. Breakfast and lunch. This meat and three is a Nashville favorite, with the fried chicken being almost as good as what I used to get at my grandmother's. Also great are the roast beef that is on the menu every day, along with pies that are perennial winners at the state fair. Owner Jack Arnold has been a friend to many of the celebrities—you might even see people like Chet Atkins and George "Goober" Lindsey chowing down at Arnold's. It's a small restaurant—the kind of place where other lunchers are not shy about sitting down with you if you have a spare seat. It's been open since the early eighties. 256-4455.

• Belle Meade Cafeteria, 4534 Harding Road in the Belle Meade Plaza Shopping Center. This Nashville tradition, a lunch and dinner cafeteria, is always a good bet. In business since 1961, it has great vegetables. Open Monday through Saturday, 11:00 A.M. to 2:00 P.M. and from 4:30 P.M. to 8:00 P.M.; on Sunday from 10:30 A.M. until 8:00 P.M. The prices are already reasonable, but check the senior specials if you're old enough. 298-5571.

• BellSouth Cafeteria, in the BellSouth Building at 323 Commerce Street downtown. This is a great but little known choice for an inexpensive and quick downtown breakfast or lunch. Breakfast is served (and the public is welcome) from 6:45 A.M. to 10:15 A.M. and lunch is from 11:00 A.M. to 1:30 P.M. Most lunches, consisting of an entrée,

NASHVILLE CELEBRITY INSIDER'S TIP

George "Goober" Lindsey recommends: "Dotson's in Franklin for the vegetables. And they even have banana pudding. I've been eating there since college. I went to college at North Alabama in Florence and it's pretty similar now. I'm a vegetable plate man.

"I also love the Belle Meade Buffet cafeteria. I get the vegetable plate there. And I like Demos. Nashville has some awful good restaurants."

(Continued on next page)

two vegetables, and a roll, are in the sub-$4 range. There is also a daily grill special and a daily deli special in the same price range. 742-0261.

• Big River Grille and Brewing Works, 111 Broadway. You might be pushing the limit here, with sandwiches running around $6, but there are some cheaper salads and other items. Hardly anything is over $10 at this downtown brew pub. They have pool tables and darts for your entertainment. Open from 11:00 A.M. to 11:00 P.M., seven days a week. 251-4677. $$

• Blue Moon Waterfront Cafe, 525 Basswood Avenue. You might have to order carefully to come in around $6 here, but this place is a treat, maybe even worth a splurge. 352-5892. $$

• Bobbie's Dairy Dip, 5301 Charlotte Avenue. This fifties drive-in is mainly known for its ice cream and people watching, but the food is respectable, too. One of my readers heartily recommends the white beans, which cost 50¢ for a sixteen-ounce cup on Wednesdays. Wednesday is the day to eat here, with specials including pimiento cheese sandwiches for 50¢ and a foot-long hot dog with mustard, onion, and relish for $1. Even on other days, the prices are great with a polish sausage sandwich, fries, and drink being $3.39 or homemade low-fat chicken salad and baked chips for around $3. The Dip is open from 10:00 A.M. to 9:00 P.M. Monday through Thursday; and 10:00 A.M. to 10:00 P.M., Friday and Saturday. Closed Sunday. 385-4661.

Lindsey figures that when it comes to entertainment, you can get the most for your money at the Grand Ole Opry or the shows at the Ryman Auditorium. "You get a lot for what you pay."

"Another place is the Parthenon. It's only $2.50 and you can see Athena and all the rest. Cheekwood is only $5 and you can see a lot there. It's a great value. There's a lot in Nashville. You can have an inexpensive vacation here."

• Bongo Java, 2007 Belmont Boulevard. This is really a coffee house but also a fine place for a sandwich. A favorite choice is called a Pesto Bomb, but they also have other bagel-type sandwiches, vegetarian and otherwise. Prices are very moderate. The kitchen is open from 7:00 A.M. until 11:00 P.M. 385-5282.

• Bread and Company's two locations are 4105 Hillsboro Road (292-7323) and 106 Page Road (352-7323). They come in just under Ms. Cheap's price limit, with sandwiches $4–$6 and soups starting at about $3.50. They also have salads. This is really a bakery first and a cafe second, but the lunch food gets good reviews. Hours are 7:00 A.M. until 6:00 P.M.

• Bro's Cajun Cuisine, 5207 Nolensville Road, is owned and operated by Darrell Breaux. This Cajun eat-in or take-out joint has red beans and rice and étouffée, served in huge portions. Prices range from $2.50 to $6.50

for most things. Open Monday from 11:00 A.M. to 2:30 P.M., and from 11:00 A.M. to 8:00 P.M. Tuesday through Saturday. Closed Sunday. 834-8777.

• Brown's Diner, 2102 Blair Boulevard. Brown's is known as one of Nashville's top hamburger havens. Nothing fancy, for sure, but great juicy burgers in a beer joint atmosphere. It's very consistent. Burgers are under $3, and the most expensive item on the menu is the $4.50 catfish dinner. The kitchen is open Monday through Saturday, 11:00 A.M. to 10:30 P.M.; Sunday, noon to 10:00 P.M. 269-5509.

• Calypso Cafe, with three locations: 21 Arcade (259-9631), 2424 Elliston Place (321-3878), and on Thompson Lane just across from 100 Oaks Shopping Mall (297-6530). This place is described as a "Caribbean meat and three." It's actually a meat and two with about half of the entrées between $5 and $6 and half between $4 and $5. It is definitely a good value for very good food served in fairly generous portions. Try the chicken, greens (called Callaloo), and Cuban black beans for a good sample of what they can do. Elliston Place and Thompson Lane serve lunch and dinner, and the Arcade location has lunch only. I have a pal who recommends ordering the large black bean salad and splitting it with a friend.

• Carolyn's Homestyle Kitchen, 330 Charlotte Avenue. This downtown meat and three at the corner of Fourth and Charlotte Avenues is the real thing, with a meat, two vegetables, and bread coming in under $5. The fried chicken, green beans, and real mashed potatoes that we wolfed down recently were perfect. It is open from 10:00 A.M. until 1:55 P.M. weekdays. If you go on Friday, fish day, expect to wait. 255-1008.

• Chez Jose, 2323 Elliston Place. Open Monday through Thursday, 11:00 A.M. to 9:00 P.M.; Friday and Saturday, until 10:00 P.M.; Sunday, noon to 7:00 P.M. This relatively new Vanderbilt-area spot is self-serve, limited-menu Mexican—quesadillas, burritos, tacos, etc. The chicken tacos are out of this world. There is even a salsa bar with six different kinds of salsa ranging from mild to too hot to handle. Chez Jose was an instant hit with Nashville eaters, maybe because it's good, cheap, and even not too bad for your health. 320-0107.

• Clayton-Blackmon, 4117 Hillsboro Road in Green Hills. I recommend the rollers (veggie or high roller, which are about $5) as well as sandwiches and the low-fat chicken salad, which are also about $5. Individual salads start at $1.45 a portion so you could get three salads within the limit. 8:30 A.M. to 7:00 P.M., Monday through Friday; and 8:30 A.M. to 6:00 P.M. on Saturday. Closed Sunday. 297-7855.

• Center Point Barbecue, 1212 West Main Street in Hendersonville. Center Point, which has been in business since 1965, is known as one of Middle Tennessee's very best barbecue restaurants. Not fancy, just good lean barbecue with good sauce. Owners Bill and Bonnie Loyd are almost as proud of their clientele as they are of their barbecue. Their place has been a favorite with the country stars, if the walls are telling the truth. There are autographed pictures of stars everywhere—Johnny Cash, Conway Twitty, Porter Wagoner, Jerry Reed, Billy Walker, etc. Mary Chapin Carpenter was quoted in *Bon Appétit* magazine as saying it was one of her favorite places to eat. 824-9330.

• Corner Market, in the Westgate Shopping Center at the intersection of Highway 70 and Highway 100. This upscale market still has affordable items on the menu, like the Eclectic Salad or the half-sandwich and cup of soup. Side salads are $1.50. Hours are 8:30 A.M. to 7:00 P.M., Monday through Friday; 10:00 A.M. to 7:00 P.M. on Saturday; noon to 7:00 P.M. on Sunday. 352-6772.

• Dan's Cafe, 538 Lafayette, offers breakfast and lunch and has been reviewed as "southern food at its best" for its lunches. Dan's is known for its vegetables such as turnip greens, green beans, sweet potatoes, broccoli, cheese, etc., and meats such as braised pork chops and fried fish (on Friday). The cornbread muffins are also popular. Checks are accepted but no credit cards. Open 6:00 A.M. to 2:00 P.M. 256-8501.

• DaVinci's Gourmet Pizza, 1812 Hayes Street. These are definitely gourmet pizzas, with ingredients such as blue cheese, potatoes, oysters, spinach, etc. The price might seem high but when you figure how many people a pie will feed, it comes

NASHVILLE EATS

Nicki Pendleton, renowned area restaurant critic, has six favorites:

1. Joe's for Barbecue. *"Cooked over a real pit, Joe's is as good as any barbecue in the mid-state. Variety is the spice of life here, with chopped chicken, pork, or beef brisket available on buns or cornbread, as dinners or in quantity."* 3716 Clarksville Highway. 259-1505.

2. Amy's. *"For a fresh cheap lunch."* 500 Church Street. 242-2697.

3. Interasian Market and Deli. *"For the $3 Vietnamese noodle bowls. When I get a hankering for Asian food, this is where I go. Strictly fresh ingredients, dishes prepared one at a time, not dished from one huge pot. The quality makes up for the very limited menu. Get the noodle bowls or the bahn cuon, [steamed spring roll-type thing]."* 2181 Nolensville Road. 742-3268.

(Continued on next page)

out as a bargain. Whole pizzas range from $11.25 to $21.95 depending on size and ingredients. Hours are 4:30 P.M. to 10:00 P.M., Sunday through Thursday; 4:30 P.M. to 10:30 P.M., Friday and Saturday; closed Monday. 329-8098.

• Davis-Kidd Booksellers' Second Story Cafe, 4007 Hillsboro Road in Green Hills. Open 11:00 A.M. to 9:00 P.M., Monday through Saturday, serving sandwiches, salads, and great desserts. Even the bookstore manager says it's fudging to say you can eat for under $6 but it is too close. Maybe under $7 would get it. I never thought I'd recommend a chicken pot pie but the hearty one here is superb. 385-0043. $$

• Demos Steak and Spaghetti, 300 Commerce Street. Lunch here is a real bargain if you get the daily special. It's only $3.95 and comes with salad or soup. Almost everything on the lunch menu is under $6, and even at dinner there are some under-$6 options such as spaghetti. Open 11:00 A.M. to 11:00 P.M., Sunday through Thursday; 11:00 A.M. to midnight, Friday and Saturday. This is right on the fringe of the District and Second Avenue, so it is very convenient for downtown visitors. 256-4655.

NASHVILLE EATS

4. The Blue Chip Salad at Garden Allegro. *"This sunny vegetarian natural foods restaurant offers made-from-scratch offerings that even a meat eater could love. Tofu sloppy Joes, vegetarian curry, steamed veggies, spinach lasagna, a daily bean dish, and a daily fish."* 1805 Church Street. 327-3834.

5. Catfish on Friday at Carolyn's Homestyle Kitchen. 330 Charlotte Avenue. 255-1008.

6. The panini at Owl's Nest. *"It [the panini, which is a split focaccia brushed with oil and filled with meat or cheese or vegetables and cooked] could easily turn into a fetish item, like Gold Rush's bean roll, Brown's Diner's hamburger, or Mosko's Looney Tuna, a thing people crave."* 205 Twenty-second Avenue North. 321-2771.

• Elliston Place Soda Shop, 2111 Elliston Place, with fifties atmosphere and good diner food for breakfast, lunch, and dinner, has been in business since 1939. Plate lunches are $4.99, with the most popular being Thursday's turkey and dressing. The most ordered sandwich is the hot roast beef, $4.99. The most expensive thing on this menu is the rib eye steak at $6.45. Hours are 6:00 A.M. to 7:45 P.M. 327-1090.

• Elvy's, 891 Elm Hill Pike. This lunch-only deli, which has been making sandwiches since 1989, is nice and clean and has a daily special that includes a whole sandwich, chips, and drinks for under $5, including tax. The fare is mostly sandwiches and soups. On the regular menu, the most expensive sandwich is $4.55 with tax. Open 9:00 A.M. to 3:00 P.M., Monday through Friday. 244-3589.

• Farmers Market at the edge of the Bicentennial Mall has five choices for lunch: the Mad Platter Deli, Swett's, Cafe Elliston, the Gyro Shop,

■ *Ms. Cheap's Quick-Saving Tip:*

Order water when you eat out.

and Island Spice. All offer lunch choices for under $6. It's a lot of fun to walk around before or after your lunch. Restaurant hours vary but the market is open from 9:00 A.M. to 6:00 P.M., Sunday through Friday; from 8:00 A.M. to 7:00 P.M. on Saturday. 880-2001.

• Fat Mo's, with three locations: 2620 Franklin Road (298-1111), 946 Richards Road (781-1830), and 1216 Murfreesboro Road (366-3171). Lunch and dinner. Advertising itself as having "hamburgers like they were before fast food," this take-out hamburger joint makes a giant juicy burger. Even the Baby Mo is a big lunch for normal people. The Fat Mo Super Deluxe contains more than twenty-seven ounces, enough to "feed a family," Mo says. One local restaurant reviewer has called it a "beef buzz." Fat Mo's also has milk shakes and fries, roast beef sandwiches, chicken strips, and onion rings. Open 10:00 A.M. to 10:00 P.M. Suggestion: Call in your order if you are in a hurry.

• Fletcher's Pizza, 2500 Lebanon Road. This Donelson institution is a big-eater pleaser for sure, with an all-you-can-eat lunch buffet of pizza, spaghetti, salad, and bread for $3.19. "Nobody can beat our prices," owner Harry Fletcher says. The buffet is in effect from 11:00 A.M. to 2:00 P.M. every day but Saturday, as well as on Tuesday night from 5:00 to 8:00 P.M. If you want to order from the menu, it is still a good deal, with sandwiches starting at $1.59 and with the largest, most-loaded pizza coming in under $10. Fletcher's has been in business since 1978. Hours are 11:00 A.M. to 11:00 P.M. on weeknights; 11:00 A.M. to midnight on Friday and Saturday. 883-1844.

• Gerst Haus, on Woodland Street across the river from downtown near the new football stadium, this fun and friendly German restaurant is a Nashville institution. Nearly all of the sandwiches are under $6 (I like the Reuben) and nothing on the menu is too high. The Gerst Haus has been in business since 1954, starting downtown and then moving across the river. The owners (who also own the two Sportsman's Grille restaurants) were planning on moving the Gerst again sometime in 1997 or early 1998 to accommodate the new stadium. So call to find out the latest before you go. Hours are 11:00 A.M. to 11:00 P.M. daily, and there is a German oompah band on Saturday from 5:30 to 10:00 P.M. 256-9760.

• Gold Rush, 2205 Elliston Place. Known for the bean roll, this more-than-twenty-year-old restaurant has lots of priced-right items to choose from, such as burgers and wings. Open 11:00 A.M. to midnight, Monday through Friday; from 5:00 P.M. to midnight on Saturday and Sunday. 327-2809. $$

• Goldie's Deli, in the Belle Meade Plaza Shopping Center. Formerly known as Schwartz's Delicatessen, it has great sandwiches for take-out or eat-in. All meats are kosher. Among the most popular sandwiches are the Reuben and the fresh turkey breast, both of which are under $5. Goldie's is open from 9:30 A.M. to 5:00 P.M., Monday through Saturday; from 9:30 A.M. to 3:00 P.M. on Sunday. 292-3589.

• Green Hills Cafeteria, in the Retired Teachers Building in Green Hills, 2209 Abbott Martin Road. Come in the back entrance and find a nice cafeteria with prices that make Ms. Cheap smile—a meat and three vegetables for less than $5, including bread. There's roast beef and real mashed potatoes every day. Open Monday through Friday from 11:00 A.M. to 2:00 P.M. for lunch; from 4:30 to 7:00 P.M. for dinner. 292-1366.

• Hard Rock Cafe, 100 Broadway. You might think it's expensive, but it really isn't. A burger and fries can squeeze under my $6 limit or you can go cheaper with a bowl of chili or soup. Friday breakfast (7:00 to 9:00 A.M.) is the real deal here, which is $3 or $4 for a hot breakfast buffet, live radio broadcast, and sometimes live music. See locals hang out. 742-9900.

• Henry's Great Coffee House, 318 Broadway. There is a $3.99 breakfast buffet of omelets, Belgian waffles, etc., every day from 7:00 to 10:00 A.M. on weekdays; from 10:00 A.M. to 2:00 P.M. on weekends. Every day there is a lunch special of a deli sandwich, soup or salad, cookies, and a drink for $4.99; and there is a $2.99 soup and salad bar. Friday is pizza day with a personal pizza special. Hours are complicated: Monday, from 7:00 A.M. to 10:00 P.M.; Tuesday through Thursday, from 7:00 A.M. to midnight; Friday from 7:00 A.M. to 1:00 A.M.; Saturday, from 10:00 A.M. to 1:00 A.M.; and Sunday, from 10:00 A.M. to 10:00 P.M. 742-6343.

■ *Ms. Cheap's Quick-Saving Tip:*

When you go out to eat, split dinners when you can. Lots of time there is plenty for two if you just order an extra salad. Or, order two full meals and plan to doggy bag some of each for a "free" meal later at home.

• Hog Heaven, 115 Twenty-seventh Avenue North, right next to Centennial Park, is an obvious choice for a Parthenon/Centennial Park picnic. Sandwiches and barbecue plates. Pork, chicken, turkey, and brisket are the offerings, along with turnip greens, black-eyed peas, corn, green beans, and white beans. The barbecue is fabulous. If you want something different, you might want to sample the white sauce with the chicken. Open 10:00 A.M. to 7:00 P.M., Monday through Saturday. Closed Sunday. Also sells barbecue by the pound and will deliver within a limited service area. Sandwiches are $3 and $4, while plates are between $5 and $6. 329-1234.

• International Market, 2010-B Belmont Boulevard. Open 9:00 to 9:00, seven days a week, this is both a market and a restaurant. The restaurant offers a cafeteria line with several choices of authentic Thai cuisine as well as some Chinese dishes. There's not much to be said about the atmosphere, but the food is good and the price is right. One of this place's biggest fans says to order the food to go, and they will give you more. He says he orders rice, two of the entrées, and a cucumber salad for just about $5. For dessert, he suggests a White

NASHVILLE EATS

Susan Chappell, critic for *Nashville Life* magazine, lists her five favorites:

1. Sitar. *"The all-you-can-eat lunch buffet is hard to beat for $5.95. I eat whatever is on tap for the day."* 116 Twenty-first Avenue North. 321-8889.

2. Mary's. *"The smell alone is enough to make my car automatically turn into this place. I usually order a shoulder sandwich. Corncakes are hard to pass up."* 1108 Jefferson. 256-7696.

3. The International Market. *"The Pad Thai isn't on the menu, but they will make it with either chicken or shrimp, if you ask. Add some papaya juice and you have a filling meal."* 2010-B Belmont Boulevard. 297-4453.

4. La Hacienda Taqueria. *"I go for the hefty chicken burrito which is quite filling, especially when paired with the chips and salsa."* 5560 Nolensville Road. 833-3716.

(Continued on next page)

Rabbit taffy-like candy for a nickel. Oh, and don't get mixed up and go to the International House across the street. It is pretty pricey. 297-4453.

NASHVILLE EATS

5. Corner Market. *"I'm addicted to the Corner Market's Eclectic Salad with strawberries, blue cheese, avocado, and their terrific sesame dressing."* Westgate Shopping Center. 352-6772.

• Jack's Barbecue, 416 Broadway. This lunch and dinner spot, which has a patio at the back door of the Ryman Auditorium, is a good place for a sandwich and a cold beer or drink at lunch or late afternoon. Sandwiches start under $3 and plates are just over $6. Owner Jack Cawthon has been serving barbecue to Nashville for more than twenty years. Open 10:30 A.M. to 10:00 P.M. 254-5715.

• Joe's Barbecue, 3716 Clarksville Highway. This has been rated the best barbecue in town in some surveys. They serve chicken, pork, and beef barbecue as well as ribs. It's open 10:30 A.M. to 10:00 P.M. on weekdays and a little later on weekends. Closed Sunday. 259-1505.

• Knowles Senior Citizens Center, 1801 Broadway. Open from 11:30 A.M. to 1:00 P.M., this cafeteria is great with a meat and two vegetables adding up to about $3. Desserts and cups of soup are 60¢, and where else can you get a cup of coffee for 30¢? The public is welcome. 327-4551.

• La Hacienda Taqueria, 2615 Nolensville Road. This might be my favorite cheap place to eat in Nashville. You almost feel like you are in Mexico when you come here. I suggest either the chicken burrito or getting two of the beef tacos for lunch. If you ask, you get free chips, a nice bowl of salsa, and a water with lime. The food is brought to you on real plates (not Styrofoam or paper) and a goodly percentage of the other guests are Hispanic. The adjoining grocery is a fun place to look around before or after your lunch or dinner. Open 9:00 to 9:00 daily. 256-6142. Two other locations are at 1019 Gallatin Road in Madison and at 5560 Nolensville Road (in the Wal-Mart Center at Old Hickory Boulevard).

• Loveless Restaurant, 8400 Highway 100. Another Nashville tradition and worth the drive if you like country ham, fried chicken, and scratch biscuits. Owner Donna McCabe says even though the dinners of country ham and fried chicken exceed Ms. Cheap's limit, a lot of her customers order à la carte and come in under $6 for a good meal. Expect to wait once you get to this restaurant, unless you have reservations, especially on the weekends. Seniors get a 10 percent discount, if you ask. Breakfast, lunch, and dinner. Open 8:00 A.M. to 2:00 P.M. and 5:00 to 9:00 P.M., Monday through Friday, and from 8:00 A.M. until 9:00 P.M. on Sunday. 646-9700. $$

• Mack's Cafe, 2009 Broadway. This seventy-seven-year-old restaurant's best selling item is the hot roast beef sandwich served with mashed potatoes ($4.75). They serve a lot of plate lunches, too, and are open from 10:30 A.M. to 3:00 P.M., Monday through Friday. Mack's is also open at night with a limited menu and music. 327-0700.

• Major Brew, 1900 Broadway. This beer store/market, whose slogan is "Beer is not just for breakfast anymore," offers a good selection of big sandwiches at lunch. They also have soup in the autumn and winter months. Nothing is more than $5. They feature one biggy sandwich called the Triple Double which is the top of the line, all the way down to a lowly bologna sandwich. Call ahead and put in your order if you don't want to wait. Lunch is hectic. There is some seating but most of the business is to go. Hours for the deli are 11:00 A.M. to 4:00 P.M. 321-3363.

• Mama Mia's, 4671 Trousdale. At lunch, Mama Mia's is a deal but at dinner it is a little too pricey for Ms. Cheap. Lunch is from 11:00 A.M. to 2:00 P.M., Monday through Friday, and most items start at $4 and go up. Spaghetti, calzone, ravioli, and sandwiches are all under $6 at lunchtime. 331-7207.

• Market Street Brewery and Public House, 134 Second Avenue North. This brew pub, where they make the Market Street beer products, is in the heart of the District. It would make a good stop for lunch or a light dinner, especially if you are a beer connoisseur. Hours are 11:00 to 11:00 weekdays, and from 11:00 A.M. to midnight on weekends. 259-9611.

• Mary's Old Fashion Bar-B-Que, 1108 Jefferson Street. This is the queen of Nashville's barbecue places, featuring barbecue pork, chicken, and ribs. Sandwiches are under $3 and plates are $4 to $5. Mary's has been a fixture for almost thirty years. Open twenty-four hours, seven days a week. 256-7696.

• McCabe Pub, 4410 Murphy Road. This is a burger, meat and three, and salad family place that can take care of everybody at lunch and dinner and squeeze within our budget. There are some entrées in the $8 and $9 range but plenty of choices for under $6. Open 11:00 A.M. until midnight, seven days a week. 269-9406.

• Menu Express. If you want food delivered, here is your deliverer. Menu Express is tied in with a number of

Nashville's good restaurants and will bring your order to your home or hotel room. The delivery area is limited but it's worth a call. 367-3663. (Take-out Taxi is a similar service: 383-5333.)

• The Merchants Restaurant, 401 Broadway. Dinner is over the budget but there are some great lunch deals in the $3.99 to $5.99 range. If you like a historic setting and contemporary food, this is a good downtown lunch bet. Open 11:00 A.M. to 2:30 P.M., Monday through Friday. Dinners start at about $9. 254-1892.

• Mère Bulles, 152 Second Avenue North. At lunch you can almost always eat for under $6. Lunch is served between 11:00 A.M. and 4:00 P.M., with sandwiches, soups, and salads all under $6, although at dinner it might be too expensive. 256-1946.

• Mighty Chicken and Fixings, 1305 Jefferson Street. This is the place for wings. They have Cajun wings, buffalo wings, herb wings, sweet and sour wings, Mexican wings, and teriyaki wings. You can get an eight-piece, twelve-piece,

NASHVILLE EATS

Kay West, critic for the *Nashville Scene*, has a top-five list:

1. Prince Hot Chicken Shack. *"A peculiar Nashville delicacy, Hot Chicken gets its identity from the spice level, not the temperature. Chicken is dredged through a mixture of flour, spices, and cayenne pepper, then fried to a dark crisp in lard in a black iron skillet. Order it by the piece, a half or whole chicken, mild, medium hot, or extra hot. It comes with white bread and pickles. The mild is an eye opener, the medium will clear your sinuses, the hot makes grown men cry, and the extra hot is only for the seriously disturbed. Use caution while eating—wash your hands before touching your eye or any sensitive tissue. Soothe the fire with noncarbonated beverages like iced tea, lemonade, or water or you might explode."* 123 Ewing Drive. 226-9442.

(Continued on next page)

sixteen-piece deal on up to one hundred pieces, depending on what you want. They also have whiting and catfish sandwiches, burgers, chicken sandwiches, and tenders, all very reasonably priced, and all kinds of side items at 99¢ each. It's eat-in or take-out. Open from 11:00 A.M. until 1:00 A.M., Monday through Thursday; 11:00 A.M. until 3:30 A.M. on Friday and Saturday; and from 4:00 to 10:00 P.M. on Sunday. 327-8005.

• Milano's Pizzeria in Brentwood, at 5008 Maryland Farms Way. This little restaurant has a special featuring two slices of pizza and a drink, or a slice of pizza, salad, and drink for $2.99. That's hard to beat, especially since it is good pizza and a pretty presentable salad. Milano's is open from 10:30 A.M. to 9:00 P.M. on weekdays; from 11:30 A.M. to 9:00 P.M. on Saturday; and from 4:30 to 9:00 P.M. on Sunday. 373-8200.

• Monell's, 1235 Sixth Avenue North. This one exceeds Ms. Cheap's limit but it is too good not to include. This restaurant, housed in an 1840s home in Germantown, serves its food

NASHVILLE EATS

2. La Hacienda Taqueria. *"La Hacienda Taqueria began life as a combination Mexican grocery store/tortilla factory. A grill and a few tables were added first, and then a major expansion took place that removed the tortilla factory to another location and replaced it with about twenty small tables. The menu is in Spanish, the cooks and servers are Mexican, and you cannot count on them to be bilingual. Soft tacos are served with a slice of fresh avocado, lime, and plenty of fresh chopped cilantro. Sample the shrimp salad while enjoying the Mexican videos on the television. Take a bag of tortilla chips and salsa to go."* 2615 Nolensville Road. 256-6142.

3. Chez Jose. *"Mexican food without the guilt or the fatty, greasy, cheesy hangover that makes you feel like you swallowed a whole piñata. Grilled veggies,*

(Continued on next page)

family style, meaning you sit at a table with whoever else happens to be hungry that day. It's all you can eat (without embarrassing yourself) with different menus each day: Tuesday and Friday, fried chicken; Thursday, country-fried steak; Wednesday, meat loaf. It's one price—$7—and it even includes a dessert and iced tea. My favorite is the chicken, and all of the vegetables I have had were like those I used to get at my grandmother's. The offerings each day include one entrée, four vegetables, two salads, dessert, bread, and tea. Monell's is open 11:00 A.M. to 2:30 P.M. for lunch and from 5:00 to 8:00 P.M. for supper. Saturday morning breakfast is served from 8:00 A.M. to noon, and Sunday dinner from 11:00 A.M. to 3:00 P.M. 248-4747. $$

• Mosko's Muncheonette, 2204 Elliston Place. Open 7:00 A.M. to 4:00 P.M. Monday through Friday, and 8:30 A.M. to 4:00 P.M., Saturday and Sunday. The Muncheonette serves great sandwiches (half or whole) and salads, The store sells almost everything—great greeting cards, an assortment of interesting

NASHVILLE EATS

chicken, beef, shrimp, or catch of the day in a flour or corn tortilla or as a platter with steamed rice and meaty black beans. The guacamole is muy bueno. Order a bowl of chips and sample the salsa bar—six varieties from mild to flaming." 2323 Elliston Place. 320-0107.

4. Farmers Market. "Nashville's new (1996) Farmers Market has plenty of what you would expect—fruits and vegetables from local growers and plants, greenery, and flowers from nearby nurseries. But step inside the newest section of the market and take a trip around the world. Fried Jamaican meat patties, gyros and hummus, Italian panini sandwiches, fried chicken and turnip greens, and Nashville's best Reuben at the Mad Platter Deli are all on the internationally inclined menu available from the interior booths at the market. And don't forget to take home a bag of home-grown tomatoes or a big orange pumpkin." 900 Eighth Avenue North. 880-2001.

(Continued on next page)

beers, lots of cigars, and all kinds of newspapers. The motto is "Eat it, read it, smoke it." It's a fun place to browse as well as eat. 327-2658.

NASHVILLE EATS

5. The Gerst Haus.
"You could drink a couple of the fish bowl-sized icy-cold draft beers for under $6. Or get one beer and indulge in a Bavarian pizza, kielbasa sandwich, or the traditional oyster roll, definitely an acquired habit. One of Nashville's oldest and most enduring beer halls and courthouse/city hall hangouts, the Gerst Haus will not survive the wrecking ball when it comes time to clear the east-side river properties for Nashville's new professional football stadium. Pay a visit while you can." 228 Woodland Street. 256-9760.

• Nashville Country Club, 1811 Broadway. This restaurant offers coupons in the daily newspapers and the *Nashville Scene* that bring the price down to a true-value level, at lunch or dinner. Some of the sandwiches and most of the appetizers squeeze by in the under-$6 range. Open Monday through Thursday, 11:00 A.M. to 10:00 P.M.; Friday, until 11:00 P.M.; Saturday from 9:00 A.M. to 11:00 P.M.; and Sunday from 10:00 to 10:00. 321-0066. $$

• New York Bagel, 3009 West End Avenue. This is a great spot for breakfast, and equally good for lunch, in the Vanderbilt/West End area. There are several other New York Bagel locations around town that should be a good bet as well. Open 6:00 A.M. to 8:00 P.M., Monday through Saturday, and 7:00 A.M. to 5:00 P.M. on Sunday. 329-9599.

• Nick's Italian Deli, 508 Fifth Avenue South. Open 10:30 A.M. until 4:00 P.M. This is a deal if I ever saw one, with hot pasta dishes, such as spaghetti and meatballs, chicken parmigiana, lasagna, or eggplant parmigiana, served with bread and salad for under $5. Nick's also has cold platters and great sandwiches, hot or cold, for around or under $4. 254-7210.

• Nooley's, 118 Royal Oaks Boulevard in Franklin. This is known for its Cajun food and po-boys, with almost everything on the menu being under $6. It's étouffée, gumbo, red beans and rice, shrimp, roast beef, and turkey po-boys. Open 10:30 A.M. to 8:00 P.M. every day but Sunday. This is just off the I-65/Highway 96 exit in Franklin. 790-6019.

• Obie's, 2217 Elliston Place. This is one of Nashville's most popular pizzerias, with pizza being sold by the piece or by the pie. Open 11:00 A.M. to 2:00 P.M. and 5:00 to 10:00 P.M. during the week, and until midnight on the weekend. 327-4772.

• The Old Spaghetti Factory, 160 Second Avenue North. This might be the best deal in town for good food (and lots of it) at a reasonable price in a good atmosphere. At night, meals include salad, bread, drink, and dessert, along with the pasta, for a fixed price that runs as little as $5 to $6. Lunch, which is pasta, salad, and bread (no drink or dessert), starts at $3.25 and goes up to a little over $5. Open Monday through Friday from 11:30 A.M. to 2:00 P.M. and 5:00 to 10:00 P.M.; Saturday from noon to 11:00 P.M.; from 4:00 to 10:00 P.M. on Sunday. 254-9010.

• Opryland Hotel has a food court in the Delta that fits Ms. Cheap's under-$6-per-meal budget. There are six outlets offering assorted foods such as pizza, Chinese, burgers, and salads. This is a good deal, with plenty to look at as you eat on the scenic indoor riverbank. Lunch only. 889-1000.

• Owl's Nest, 205 Twenty-second Avenue North. This is really a coffee house but lots of people go to eat. There is a daily special featuring a panini (Italian bread sandwich) with soup and a drink for $5, including tax. The nest is open from 7:00 A.M. until midnight, Monday through Wednesday; from 7:00 A.M. until 1:00 A.M. on Thursday and Friday; and from 11:00 A.M. until midnight on Saturday. Closed Sunday. 321-2771.

• Pancake Pantry, 1796 Twenty-first Avenue South. This restaurant's reputation is built on breakfast, where you will find a long wait most weekend mornings. It

■ *Ms. Cheap's Quick-Saving Tip:*

Consider ordering an appetizer instead of an entrée if you are not really that hungry. Often it will be creative, good, and offer plenty of food.

also serves lunch, which is a good value as well. Open 6:00 A.M. to 5:00 P.M., seven days a week, serving breakfast all day. Burgers and the famous dipper are good lunch sellers, both just under $6. There is also the create-your-own sandwich that starts at about $4 and goes up as you add items. 383-9333.

• The Pie Wagon, 118 Twelfth Avenue South. This hearty breakfast spot and meat-and-three lunch is a good cheap bet on weekdays. It's about halfway between downtown and Music Row. A meat and three veggies is under $6 every day. Sandwiches start at about $2 and go up to about $3.50. Open 6:00 to 10:30 A.M. for breakfast and 10:30 A.M. to 2:00 P.M. for lunch, Monday through Friday. 256-5893.

• Pizza Perfect. There are two locations (4002 Granny White Pike, 297-0345; and 1602 Twenty-first Avenue South, 329-2757) and the menus are almost identical. However, they are separately owned and operated. Pizza is the main business but they also have burgers, calzones, pastas, and sandwiches, as well as one of the best Italian salads in town. Pizza is sold by the slice as well as by the whole pie. Our favorite is the vegetarian that has spinach, tomato, mushrooms, and other goodies loaded on it. Granny White is open 10:00 A.M. to 11:30 P.M., Monday through Saturday. Twenty-first Avenue is open 11:00 A.M. until midnight daily.

• Planet Hollywood, 322 Broadway. It's hard for Ms. Cheap to find something here within her budget, but it is a fun experience to just look around. The cheapest hamburger is $6.95 but you could order soup or salad and come in on the low side. Open 11:00 A.M. until midnight, seven days. 322-STAR. $$

• Pop's Bar B Q, at 701B Twenty-eighth Avenue North. You need to know where you are going because the sign is hardly visible. If you find Swett's at the corner of Twenty-eighth and Clifton, look catty-cornered across the street in a small strip center and Pop's is right in the middle. It's barbecued beef, pork, chicken, rib tips, sausage, bologna, and even goat. There are sandwiches and plates that are served with vegetables, such as turnip greens, sweet potatoes, and potato salad. Sandwiches are under $3 and plates are under $5. Hours are Sunday through Thursday, 10:30 A.M. to 10:00 P.M.; Friday and Saturday, 10:30 A.M. until 4:00 A.M. 321-4004.

• Prince Hot Chicken Shack, 123 Ewing Lane. This hot chicken place, just off Dickerson Road at I-65, attracts both a blue- and white-collar crowd every day at lunch. The "sandwich" ($2.75) consists of two pieces of white bread, topped with hot, medium, or mild white or dark pieces of fried chicken and a toothpick full of pickles. A word of warning: At Prince's, when they say hot, they mean *hot*. We ordered the medium and it was pretty fiery. I don't think we could have managed the hot. Open noon to midnight, Tuesday through Thursday, and noon to 4:00 A.M. on Friday and Saturday. 226-9442.

• Provence Breads and Cafe, in Hillsboro Village, is really a specialty bread store that has great sandwiches and salads. It would be a fine stop for picnic fare or you can eat there and watch the activity in Hillsboro Village. Half-sandwiches are $3; side salads, about $3; soups, about $3. Pastries and breakfast items are $1.50 to $3. The bread is fabulous. They usually have samples in the front, or you can ask to taste one you might be considering for purchase. It's open 7:00 A.M. to 6:30 P.M., Monday through Thursday; 7:00 A.M. to 11:00 P.M., Friday; 8:00 A.M. to 11:00 P.M. Saturday; and 8:00 A.M. to 10:00 P.M., Sunday. 386-0363.

• Rotier's Restaurant, 2413 Elliston Place. Winner of every Nashville award for the best hamburger and cheeseburger in town, this long-standing Vanderbilt-area eatery is a must. Breakfast, lunch, and dinner. It's been in business and operated by the Rotier family for more than fifty years. Nothing on the menu exceeds the $6 mark, with the plate lunches hovering around $5. It's open 9:00 A.M. to 10:30 P.M., every day but Sunday. 327-9892.

• San Antonio Taco Company, at 416 Twenty-first Avenue South (327-4322), and San Antonio Grill, at 208 Commerce Street (259-4413) both offer a good mix of Tex-Mex options for the bargain purse. You can eat outside on a giant deck at the Twenty-first Avenue location. The most expensive thing on the menu is the chicken enchilada plate, which is about

$5, with most everything else served à la carte. Individual tacos are about $1.50. The hours at Twenty-first Avenue are Monday through Thursday, from 11:00 A.M. to midnight; Friday and Saturday, from 11:00 A.M. to 1:00 P.M.; Sunday, from 11:00 to 11:00. Downtown hours during the peak summer season are 11:00 A.M. to 10:00 P.M., Sunday through Thursday; 11:00 A.M. to midnight on Friday and Saturday. Closing times are earlier during the winter.

• Satsuma Tea Room, 417 Union Street. This is another Nashville institution, having opened in 1918 as a tearoom. It is definitely a step back in time, with good food, too. Lots of sandwiches and plates for under $5. The menu changes daily. Lunch only, 10:45 A.M. until 2:00 P.M., Monday through Friday. 256-5211.

• Siam Cafe, 316 McCall Street, just off Nolensville Road. The buffet is a bargain here (three items for under $4) , if you like Thai food. There is also a more expensive (but still reasonable) full service section of the restaurant where the food is

NASHVILLE EATS

March Egerton, author of *Adventures in Cheap Eating, Nashville and Middle Tennessee*, **also offers five personal faves:**

1. Brantley's Catfish *"in Ashland City would be right up there. It's family style and it's great."* 2905 Highway 49 West in Ashland City. 792-4703.

2. The C&J Diner. *"It's really soul food—fried chicken, pork chops, get the greens, and you gotta try the hot water cornbread."* Although there is a downtown location at 137 Seventh Avenue North, Egerton recommends the original at 405 Thirty-first Avenue North. 329-1120.

3. The Kleer-Vu in Murfreesboro *"is also soul food and is every bit as good as the C&J. And that place really rocks."* Egerton recommends steering clear of the "goofy stuff like spaghetti" and sticking with the greens, okra, chicken, and hot water cornbread. 226 South Highland. 896-0520.

(Continued on next page)

much better and more authentic Thai. Prices there range from $5 to $10. Open 11:00 A.M. to 10:00 P.M., Monday through Saturday; 5:00 to 9:00 P.M. on Sunday. It has been in business since the late 1970s. 834-3181.

NASHVILLE EATS

4. R&R Pit Bar B Q and Pub *"is a great place to get barbecue. It's sort of a tavern."* 902 North First, 227-7887.

5. La Hacienda Taqueria *"would have to be on my list. Nashville was crying out for that. Most other cities had Mexican like this but Nashville didn't."* 2615 Nolensville Road. 256-6142.

• Sitar, 116 Twenty-first Avenue North. The $5.95 lunch buffet at this Indian restaurant is hard to beat. It is a seventeen-item buffet, featuring favorite items from the nighttime menu, which is more expensive. Lunch is served from 11:00 A.M. to 2:30 P.M. Dinner, which runs between $7.95 and $12.95 per entrée, is served from 5:00 to 10:00 P.M. 321-8889.

• Sportsman's Grille, with two locations, 5405 Harding Road (356-6206), and 1601 Twenty-first Avenue South (320-1633), has a sports bar atmosphere with good grilled food. The children love the spider onion rings, and my personal favorite is the grilled chicken sandwich with Swiss cheese and bacon. Yum yum. The kitchen is open from 11:00 to 11:00 every day.

• Sunshine Grocery Natural Foods and Deli, 3201 Belmont Avenue. Salads and sandwiches in the deli—vegetarian, of course. There's also a daily special that is a soup, entrée, and drink for $4.95. Sandwiches are under $3 and the salads are anywhere from $2 a pound to $6 a pound. Open 9:00 A.M. to 7:00 P.M., Monday through Friday; 9:00 A.M. to 6:00 P.M. on Saturday. 297-5100.

• Swett's Restaurant, 2725 Clifton Avenue. This family business has won many awards for the best meat and three in town and is known for its fried chicken, turnip greens, and other vegetables. It's been in business since 1954. Lunch and dinner are offered. A meat and two runs just over $5 with a meat and three running into the $6.50 range. Open seven days a week from 11:00 A.M. to 9:00 P.M., Swett's also has a lunch-only location in Farmers Market. 329-4418.

• Sylvan Park, with three locations: 2201 Bandywood (292-6449), 4502 Murphy Road (292-2975), and 221 Sixth Avenue North (255-1562). This is a fixture in the meat-and-three category. The best one is the original on Murphy Road, which has been serving fried chicken and chocolate meringue pie since 1964. Both are out of this world. Most meat-and-two combinations are between $5 and $6. Open Monday through Saturday from 10:30 A.M. to 7:30 P.M.

• Tabouli's, 2015 Belmont Boulevard, serves chicken plates, gyro plates, and all kinds of à la carte items for under $6. Open 11:00 to 11:00, seven days a week, it's been in business since 1987. 386-0106.

• Twelfth and Porter, 114 Twelfth Avenue North. This eclectic newspaper-area restaurant, owned by Jody Faison, is a good value, with unique pizzas, pastas, burgers, salads, and stir-fries. I love the stir-fry, the black-and-blue-plate special, and the Monterrey Chicken sandwich. Twelfth and Porter has very interesting art no matter when you go. Menu prices are different at lunch and dinner with lunch being by far the best bet, with almost nothing over $6. You'd be hard-pressed to squeeze by at dinner unless you stuck with the appetizers. Open for lunch Monday through Friday, 11:30 A.M. to 2:00 P.M.; Monday through Saturday for dinner, from 5:30 P.M. until 2:00 A.M. There is also a club with music most nights and almost always a cover charge. 254-7236.

• Vandyland, 2916 West End Avenue. This Vanderbilt-area soda fountain restaurant is a throwback from the past. Owner Bea Givens describes it as "an old-time soda shop with sandwiches and ice cream." Milk shakes, sodas, sundaes, sandwiches (I love the club sandwich and the ham sandwich; the children love the grilled cheese and shakes), chicken salad, and soups. No item on the menu is more than $4.50. It is nothing fancy but always good, as is the service. The restaurant, which was originally called Candyland, has been in business since 1928. Open from 8:00 A.M. to 4:00 P.M. weekdays. 327-3868.

• Varallo's, with two downtown locations, 817 Church Street (256-9109) and 239 Fourth Avenue North (256-1907), is a chili parlor that also has plate lunches featuring home-style meats and vegetables. The mainstay is the three-way chili (about $3.50) which is chili with spaghetti and tamales. It is great on a cold day. Breakfast and lunch but no dinner. The original location is Nashville's oldest restaurant, having started in 1907. Open from 7:00 A.M. to 2:30 P.M.

• Wendell Smith's, 407 Fifty-third Avenue North (at the corner of Charlotte Avenue and Fifty-third Avenue North). This meat and three has been serving up home cooking and meat and threes for more than thirty years. Friday is the busiest day of the week, thanks to the menu choices of catfish or chicken and dressing. A meat and three vegetables runs just under $5. Hours are 6:00 A.M. to 7:30 P.M., Monday through Saturday; closed Sunday. Breakfast, lunch, and dinner. 383-7114.

• Whitt's Barbecue, with nine locations around town, is a lunch and dinner takeout kind of place featuring barbecue pork and turkey. Check it on Wednesdays when there is always a barbecue sandwich special—$1.20—that can't be beat. Check the phone book for the location (and its phone number) nearest you.

• Wolfy's, 425 Broadway. Sandwiches (the Reuben served with fries is a popular choice) and daily specials at lunch fall just under the $6 mark. Most of the menu is under $10 with the highest-priced entrée being $13.95. There is free live music every night beginning at 9:00 P.M. The kitchen is open 11:00 A.M. to midnight, seven days. 251-1621.

• Ya Mama's has two locations—605 Murfreesboro Road (251-0034), and 340 Welch Road (781-6262). Both feature home cooking in the under-$5 range for a plate.

■ Ms. Cheap's Quick-Saving Tip:

Watch and keep track of how much you save, whether you're eating, shopping, or whatever. Knowing how much I've saved helps keep me motivated. I love to look at my receipt after couponing to see how much I beat them out of. Other people I know put these savings in a big pot and use it for vacation.

e   i   g   h   t

Cheap Golf

I must admit that it was difficult for my editor (a golf nut) to convince me to include a chapter on cheap golf. To a tennis player who's accustomed to simply buying a racket and some balls and heading out to any number of free courts to play, golf seemed to be an expensive alternative.

At first blush, I couldn't find anything cheap about it. I mean, one club would cost more than my racket, balls, and water bottle put together. But after I started researching it, I found that it's all relative—that it's not necessarily cheap but maybe cheap by comparison.

And I found that memberships through Metro Parks or the state parks can make golfing pretty reasonable, especially if you are a senior. By the way, ask how old you have to be to qualify as a senior. Sometimes it's sixty-two, but a few say you're old enough at fifty. Either way, you might as well take advantage of any age-based deals.

There are some great deals available with statewide play passes, such as the Tennessee Golf Association Pass Key, the American Lung Association Lung Card, and the American Cancer Society Golf Pass that give you free greens fees on weekdays at courses in Nashville and across the state.

The Tennessee State Parks' annual statewide golf permit is particularly good for frequent players and for seniors. It's $650 a year or $325 for seniors sixty-two and older, and you can play every day on any of the state's eight public courses. In Middle Tennessee, that means Henry Horton, Montgomery Bell, Fall Creek Falls, and Old Stone Fort. The permit is good for a year from the day you buy it, so if you play a lot and like the state courses, this is the pass for you. You may purchase it at any of the state courses.

In Nashville, the best deal by far is to play on any of the six Metro golf courses. It's $8 per nine holes plus $8 for a cart, meaning two players sharing a cart would pay $12 for nine holes or $24 for eighteen holes.

Memberships for play on the Metro courses are very reasonable. Just call and ask for regular or senior (over sixty-two) prices. Call 862-8400, and ask for Special Services Division. Obviously, the cheapest of all the ways to play is to walk the course and forget the cart. On a Metro course, that makes nine holes a flat $8. That's under a dollar a hole, or even less than what the typical side bet is for weekend gamers.

The courses, which are open from dawn until dusk year-round (6:00 A.M. to 8:00 P.M. in the longest part of the summer), stay very busy and don't offer twilight or early-bird specials. Tee times for most of these courses are made seven days in advance. Here's a rundown on Metro's courses:

• The most popular is the Harpeth Hills course at 2424 Old Hickory Boulevard in Percy Warner Park, which is an eighteen-hole course with bent-grass greens. The course conditions approach the quality of lower-end country clubs. 862-8493.

• Also in the Warner Park area is the nine-hole Percy Warner course on Forrest Park Drive near Cheekwood. It has bermuda greens and is a walk-on course. 352-9958.

• The McCabe course at the corner of Forty-sixth Avenue and Murphy Road is a twenty-seven-hole course, with eighteen holes reserved by tee time and nine available for walk-on play. The course has bermuda greens. 862-8491.

• The Two Rivers course near Opryland is an eighteen-hole course with bent-grass greens. This one is popular with tourists and locals alike. 889-2675.

• The Shelby course, which is a little hard to find, is an eighteen-hole course at 2021 Fatherland Street. It has bermuda greens. To get there, go out Shelby Avenue in East Nashville to Nineteenth Street and turn left. Take a right on Fatherland and it will take you to the course. 862-8474.

• Ted Rhodes near Metro Center is located at 1901 Ed Temple Boulevard. It rates as a great course featuring bent-grass greens and an eighteen-hole layout. Ed Temple Boulevard is an extension of Eighth Avenue North. 862-8463.

• The small Riverview course at Shelby Park is a pitch-and-putt course that is open during late spring, summer, and early fall but is closed in the winter. It's $2 for adults and 75¢ for children and is a great place to practice or to help children learn. To get there, take Shelby Avenue to Seventeenth Street, turn right, and you will see it. 226-9331.

Other courses in Nashville and the midstate area that you may want to try include:

• Nashboro Village, 2250 Murfreesboro Road. This is an eighteen-hole, bent-grass-greens course. At press time it was going under new management, so call to find out what the best deals are. 367-2311.

• Hermitage, 3939 Old Hickory Boulevard has no deals. It's $34 during the week and $39 on weekends, period. It has bent-grass greens, eighteen holes. 847-4001.

• Forrest Crossing, Riverview Drive, Franklin. The regular rates here are $27 on weekdays and $37 on weekends. But if you play after 2:00 P.M., it drops to $15.50 during the week and $18.50 on the weekend. And that's with cart! Call to see if a senior rate has been added. It has bent-grass greens and is eighteen holes. 791-8100.

• Hunters Point, Lebanon. This eighteen-hole, bent-grass-greens course, has regular weekday greens fees of $9 per eighteen holes, plus $10 for a cart, meaning two people sharing a cart can play eighteen holes for $19 apiece. The same play on weekends is $23 per person. The real deal is Tuesday and Friday "senior days," when seniors can play and share a cart for $11 each. There is also a twilight special on Fridays and Saturdays after 2:30 P.M. when you can play for $14 with a shared cart. This course is in Lebanon on Highway 231 north. From Nashville, take I-40 east to exit 238, turn left, and drive about ten minutes to the course. 444-7521.

• Indian Hills, at 405 Calumet Trace in Murfreesboro, has all kinds of bargains. The regular rate for a cart and play is $25 for weekdays and $31 on weekends. But on Monday and Tuesday, there is a special $19 rate to ride and play eighteen. There is also a senior special, Monday through Friday, where seniors can ride eighteen for $17.50 or ride nine for $10.50.

College students with an ID can take advantage of the senior rate, Monday through Friday. The discount is also extended to juniors during the week and to police, firefighters, and EMT workers. There is also a weekend twilight deal during the spring, summer, and early fall, where you can play eighteen holes and ride for $19. Of course, if you walk, it is even cheaper: $7.50 for eighteen holes and $4.50 for nine. To get to Indian Hills, take I-24 to exit 81-A, and go a mile and a half to the course on the left. 898-0152.

• Old Fort Golf Course, Murfreesboro. This eighteen-hole, bent-grass-greens course has a standard $17 greens fee for eighteen holes and $9 for nine holes. A cart is $5 a person on nine holes and $8 a person on eighteen. There is a senior special, Monday through Thursday, before 10:00 A.M., when the greens fees drop to $10 for eighteen holes and $6 for nine. The discounted fees also apply to juniors (through high school) after 3:00 P.M., Monday through Thursday. The course takes tee time reservations three days in advance and also takes walk-ons on a first-come, first-served basis. From Nashville, take I-24 east to exit 78B toward Murfreesboro. Take a left on Golf Lane. 896-2448.

• Smyrna National. This eighteen-hole, bent-grass-greens course has a regular weekday or weekend green fee of $16 for eighteen holes or $8 for nine holes. Carts are $4.50 per person per nine holes. The only variance is the senior discount which is offered before 10:00 A.M., Monday through

Friday. It makes the eighteen-hole course $10 and the nine-hole course $5. To get there from Nashville, take I-24 east to exit 66B and turn east on Sam Ridley Parkway. The course is three and a half miles further on the left. 459-2666.

• Sycamore Valley, Ashland City. This eighteen-hole, bent-grass-greens course has an early bird special during the week—you can play eighteen holes and have half a cart for $20 if you start before 9:00 A.M. There is a senior special on Tuesdays until noon where you can play eighteen holes with half a cart for $17. The regular greens fees are $22 for eighteen holes and half a cart, which is really an all-day greens fee. On weekends it is eighteen holes and half a cart for $28 per person. To get there from Nashville, go I-24 west to exit 24, then left on Highway 49 for 4.7 miles. Take a left on Golf Course Lane, then left on Fox Hill to the course. 792-7863.

• Windtree, 810 Nonaville Road in Mount Juliet. Here there's a weekday $20 twilight fee, including the cart, to play all you can until dark. Times to begin vary from 1:00 to 3:30 P.M., depending on the season. This same deal is good on weekends for $22. Regular fees are $31 during the week and $36 on weekends. The course is situated off Lebanon Road in Mount Juliet. 754-4653.

• Pine Creek, 1835 Logue Road in Mount Juliet. Seniors get a break on Monday and Tuesday. If you live in Wilson County and are a member of the AARP, you get the best deal: $13.50 with the cart. If you just bring your AARP card and are not from Wilson County, it's $20. Regular weekday greens fees are $25, and weekends are $30. During the summer, there is a twilight special where you pay for nine holes ($12.50) and play as many as you can before dark. To get there, take I-40 east to the 226A exit and go one mile; turn left onto Highway 265; then go another mile to Logue Road. 449-7272.

• Country Hills, Hendersonville. This eighteen-hole, bent-grass-greens course has a senior special all day, Monday through Thursday, when eighteen holes and a cart are $20.50. The regular greens fees are $25.50 during the week and $32.50 on weekends. To get there from Nashville, take I-65 north to exit 95, follow Vietnam Veterans Parkway to Saundersville Road, turn left, and continue to the course a mile down on the left. 824-1100.

• Montgomery Bell State Park, Burns, Tennessee. Senior Day for those sixty-two years and older is every Monday and there are no greens fees. A cart is $10 a person. During the week, greens fees are $19 a day plus the cart. And on weekends, greens fees are $19 per eighteen holes plus the cart. The course is eighteen holes and has bent-grass greens. To get there from Nashville, take Highway 70 west to Burns, Tennessee. 797-2578.

• Henry Horton State Park, Chapel Hill. This is a good one: All day, Monday through Friday, the greens fees are $19, good for all day, plus cart. It's walk-on during the week. Tee times are required on the weekends when fees are $19 for eighteen holes. Monday is senior day, with seniors over sixty-two playing for free if they are Tennesseans, and for half-price if they are out-of-staters. Henry Horton also has a special $9.50 green fee, Monday through Friday, for juniors, seventeen and under. Carts are $10. (931) 364-2319.

Even the expensive courses don't have to be *sooooo* expensive:

• The Legends, Franklin. Instead of paying the regular $60 to $65 for greens fees, hold out for the after-3:00 P.M. twilight fee of $30. This won't work too well in the winter, but in the summer, it is a deal. From Nashville, go I-65 south to exit 69 west and turn right on Moores Lane to

Franklin Road. Turn left on Franklin Road and the course will be on the left. 791-8100.

• Opryland's Springhouse Golf Course, near the hotel and theme park complex, is a better bet in the winter than in the summer, with winter greens fees running $55 instead of the $62.50 and $77.50 fees during the summer. Seniors get a break in winter, too, with their fee being $42.50. Winter at Springhouse runs from November 1 to March 1. 871-7759.

Other golf deals:

• Buy a Pass Key from the Tennessee Golf Association and get one free eighteen-hole round on almost one hundred courses in the state. The card is $44.50 and is good Monday through Friday, except holidays, for greens fees. All you have to pay for is the cart. But you do need to call for a tee time and to be sure there is no conflicting tournament underway. To get a card, call the Tennessee Golf Association at 790-7600.

• Another choice is the golf privilege Lung Card from the American Lung Association of Tennessee. For $30, the card gives you free one-time greens fees at more than one hundred courses in Tennessee and Florida, with some restrictions. Call 1-800-432-LUNG in Tennessee or 1-800-329-1151 from out of state.

• And there is the American Cancer Society's Golf Pass that entitles you to one free play at more than a hundred courses in Tennessee, Kentucky, and Alabama, with some

> **■ Ms. Cheap's Quick-Saving Tip:**
>
> Use 1-800 telephone numbers whenever possible. Try 1-800-555-1212 to get directory assistance—never assume you have to pay long-distance charges.

restrictions. It's $35 and is good for one calendar year. The brochure says you can play more than three thousand holes for $35. For information, call the society office at 255-1227 or 1-800-227-2345.

• Last but not least, if you have young golfers, watch for free junior clinics. There is usually one associated with all of the big tournaments, such as the Vinny, the Sara Lee, and the BellSouth.

n i n e

Day Trips

Part of the beauty of Nashville is its central location and the fact that there is a lot to do within a few hours' drive of Nashville itself. I have listed five day trips here that are sure to be fun and all within a two-and-a-half-hour drive (some less than that). Hope you enjoy them all.

• **Drive the Tennessee Antebellum Trail.**
Middle Tennesseans and visitors can get a dose of history by visiting a number of historic homes on display along this ninety-mile loop.

There are more antebellum houses for visitors to see along the trail than in all of Mississippi, Louisiana, and

Alabama combined. So says Alton Kelley, cofounder of the Tennessee Antebellum Trail, noting that there are ninety plantations. "Most of them are fifteen hundred acres or larger, not the side-by-side city houses like in Natchez."

The houses, which served as Civil War field headquarters, hospitals, and prisoner of war quarters, range from the traditional columned houses to eighteenth-century clapboard-covered log homes to town mansions.

The trail, marked by blue-and-white signs, is not just for Civil War buffs. It also appeals to those interested in gardening, architecture, and interior decorating. The trail starts at the Belmont Mansion and runs on U.S. 31 south from Nashville to Columbia. From there, turn southwest on U.S. 243 or U.S. 412, then return to Nashville on the scenic Natchez Trace Parkway.

The *Antebellum Trail Guide* map leads visitors to fifty-four stops. Numbered plaques at each stop correspond with the guide that describes what happened there. The ideal tour companion is David Logsdon's book *Tennessee Antebellum Trail Guidebook*, which is a home-by-home, site-by-site tour book of the nineteenth-century plantations and Civil War sites.

■ *Ms. Cheap's Quick-Saving Tip:*

When you travel, take a cooler of drinks and snacks so you don't have to pay a premium for them in a market or at a fast-food joint.

"The fun of going to the old homes is learning about the stories behind them and the people who were in them and gave them personality," says Logsdon, a newspaper reporter who has published seven books on the Civil War and Maury County history.

The trail is a joint effort by tourism offices in Davidson, Williamson, and Maury Counties to lure tourists out of Nashville for a day or two. The *Tennessee Antebellum Trail Guide* is available in tourism offices in Nashville, Franklin, Maury County, and at all the open historic sites along the trail. Many of the stops are free, but others have admissions ranging from $2 to $8. For more information, call 1-800-381-1865 or 1-800-356-3445.

• Spend a day immersed in Chattanooga.

It's a two-and-a-half-hour drive southeast (down I-24) and a time change from Central time to Eastern time and it offers all kinds of options. The Tennessee Aquarium, Creative Discovery Museum, and IMAX 3-D Theater are my top picks, especially since they are conveniently located near each other so you can park and walk to all three. Also, you can get a combo ticket that gives you a price break on either two or three of the choices.

The aquarium is the world's largest freshwater aquarium and includes a sixty-foot canyon and two living forests. There are more than seven thousand animals that fly, swim, or crawl in their natural habitats. The IMAX 3-D Theater is across the street and features *Into the Deep* and two other features. The Imax show starts every hour on the hour and lasts about thirty-five minutes. With *Into the Deep*, the 3-D glasses you get on the way in, you really feel like the water and the creatures in it are in your lap. As one reviewer said, "It is as close as you can get to swimming the ocean deep without scuba gear or gills." The IMAX was added in 1996 to the $45-million freshwater facility, which has averaged one million visitors a year since opening in 1992.

Younger children, say those under ten, should also really enjoy the hands-on Creative Discovery Museum where you can dig for dinosaur bones and activate giant musical instruments.

There are plenty of places in the aquarium area where you can eat lunch. But the last time we went, we took a picnic and enjoyed the park, fountains, and manmade streams around the aquarium as a break between the IMAX movie and the aquarium. It is a very nice area, especially in the warmer months.

On your return trip to Nashville, and if you still have some energy left, a detour to Lookout Mountain and Rock City could easily be added. It really is a fun walk/hike for the whole family and the Lover's Leap overlook is breathtaking. Allow about an hour for this stop. It's open every day but Christmas. (706) 820-2531.

Other attractions in Chattanooga include:

• A shop stop would be the wonderful Warehouse Row upscale outlet shopping mall in a historic warehouse district downtown. It is two blocks from the Chattanooga Choo Choo and eight blocks from the aquarium. (423) 266-5000 or 1-800-TRACK29.

• The Chattanooga Choo Choo is a Holiday Inn hotel and restaurant complex converted from the turn-of-the-century train station in Chattanooga. There is a free shuttle between the choo choo and the aquarium area. (423) 266-5000.

• Ruby Falls, on Lookout Mountain, is a 145-foot waterfall inside Lookout Mountain Caverns. The Lookout Mountain Tower offers a panoramic view of the Tennessee Valley as well as Chattanooga. (423) 821-2544.

• The Tennessee Valley Railroad offers an authentic trip into the almost-but-not-forgotten past: a six-mile journey on a real steam-driven passenger train. Board at 4119 Cromwell Road (reached via the Jersey Pike exit off State Road 153 North) or at the East Chattanooga Station, 2200

North Chamberlain Avenue, where a railroad yard and turntable may be viewed. The fare is sort of pricey ($8.50; children ages three to twelve, $4.50), but they have a picnic area where you can bring your lunch. Days and hours for the ride vary with the season, so call (423) 751-2631.

• **Space out in Huntsville, Alabama, a two-hour drive from Nashville on I-65 south.**

The biggest attraction here is, you guessed it, the U.S. Space and Rocket Center, America's largest space attraction. The cost to visit is $14 for adults and $10 for children. The price includes admission to the museum, along with admission to Rocket Park and the sixty-seven-foot Spacedome Theater that encircles viewers. You could easily spend the whole day here operating the shuttle simulator, taking a futuristic voyage aboard the Journey-to-Jupiter simulator, and exploring the museum. There are all kinds of hands-on activities as well as the actual Apollo 16 command module. The center is open from 9:00 A.M. to 6:00 P.M. in the summer and from 9:00 A.M. to 5:00 P.M. other months. 1-800-63-SPACE. A tour of the space center could take the whole day or as little as three or four hours depending on your group.

Huntsville is really a fascinating town. It was founded in 1819 as the birthplace of Alabama. It thrived primarily as a textile town until 1950, when 118 German scientists arrived to develop rockets at Redstone Arsenal. The rest is space exploration history.

Downtown is an interesting stop with the Huntsville Depot Transportation Museum, the Alabama Constitution Village, the Huntsville Museum of Art (free), and maybe the most interesting stop—the Harrison Brothers Hardware store, which has remained virtually unchanged since it opened in 1897. It is Alabama's oldest hardware store, and it is owned and operated by the Historic Huntsville Foundation.

The Depot Trolley circles the downtown attractions. For one price you can stop and get back on as many times as you like. An even better deal is to pay $10 for a History Pass that includes admission to the village, the depot, and the trolley.

There are also several historic districts you might check out, such as the Twickenham Historic District, which is the largest concentrated area of antebellum homes in Alabama.

Another possible stop would be the 130-acre Huntsville Botanical Garden near the space center. For brochures and info on all these attractions, plus a restaurant guide, contact the Huntsville Madison County Convention and Visitors Bureau at 1-800-SPACE-4-U.

• Hohenwald

This is a different sort of shopping mecca. As Ms. Cheap, I thought I had been shopping every way you could shop: mall shopping, outlet shopping, thrift shopping, garage-sale shopping, consignment shopping, New York shopping, specialty shopping, tourist shopping, etc. Boy, was I missing the boat! I hadn't really experienced the full range of shopping until I went "dig" shopping. The dig variety takes place here in Hohenwald, which is about eighty miles

from Nashville (go to Columbia and then take Highway 412 to Hohenwald).

Two stores there—A. W. Salvage (on the hill) and Lawson's Discount Shoes and Junk Store (on the square)—specialize in digs. Here's how it works: On Wednesdays and Saturdays, just before 8:00 A.M., and on Sundays at 1:00 P.M., A. W. Salvage breaks open twelve-hundred-pound bales (sometimes one, sometimes as many as three) of clothing and spreads the contents on the floor. It looks remarkably like my daughter's room before a clean-up-your-room ultimatum. Clothes everywhere, people walking over them as though they were not there. Customers, who come from almost everywhere, line up outside the door, enter when the door opens, grab a basket or bin, and start the dig for digs.

Instead of advising you to shop till you drop, the strategy here is to drop while you shop. You literally sit in the middle of the floor and "dig" through the clothes until you find something you want. Some shoppers are looking for brands, some are looking for colors, and there are even some who are doing nothing but going through the pockets in hope of finding a lost one-hundred-dollar bill or diamond ring. (Good luck on this). In each case, the customers get excited when they find something or when they find something that goes with something they already have found.

The A. W. Salvage owner, Martha DeVandry, says about half of what is in a bale is what she would consider good, while the other half is material she ends up recycling by selling off again to other salvage vendors. But in that good half, there is a remarkable amount of branded, perfectly wearable merchandise. She won't say where the bales originate, but it is a mixture of new and used clothes, linens, and even shoes that seemingly come from thrift stores, department stores, factories, etc.

On a recent trip, my supershopper friends Marsha and Jan and I arrived just after the eight o'clock unbaling and came home midafternoon with a carload of goodies: Banana Republic pants for $3, Gap shirts for $2 each, a Nordstrom's 100-percent cotton white shirt for $2, a Benetton beach shirt at $8.99, a white damask tablecloth for $2, a pair of Umbro shorts at $1.50, Ann Taylor pants for $3—not to mention a new load of vintage and fun outfits for two of our children's "dress-up boxes."

DeVandry says despite the treasure hunt appeal, she doesn't want people to think her store is a place to get something for nothing. "We don't sell by the pound, we don't sell by the bagful," she says. "We sell by the piece, and if they are good we charge more."

She and her assistant stand at the register and evaluate and price each piece of merchandise—looking at brand name, condition, etc. They then tell the customer the price, item by item (if you ask), giving you the option of rejecting the item before it is rung up. (By the way, deciding you don't want something is pretty satisfying, too. You literally throw it back on the floor with the rest of the mess.)

Although Hohenwald is known for digging, you don't have to dig at every store. Just off the square on South Maple Street is the Outlet, which opened in 1995. It features athletic shoes, linens, and clothes. It is more of a traditional outlet, with most of its merchandise being returns or overstocked merchandise.

■ *Ms. Cheap's Quick-Saving Tip:*

Make a budget and stick to it, whether planning a big vacation or enjoying a day out on the town or in the stores.

The best deal here, we found, was in the linen and bedding section, where duvet covers were $8 and comforters were almost all under $30 (I bought one for $6). There were tablecloths and sheets as well. Individual sheets were $4 for twin, up to $7 for king, with whole sets selling for $17 at the most. But the sets go fast, the manager told us. Jeans were $8 to $15 for brands that included Levi's, Lee, Union Bay, Cherokee, etc. Shoes—Reebok, Wimbledon, and others—were in the $20-to-$30 range, with most being either new or reconditioned.

Oh, and every good shopper needs fuel, as in lunch. Choices in Hohenwald include Hardee's, McDonald's, the General Cafe, and the Rio Colorado family Mexican Restaurant and Grill. We tried the Mexican and it was great, but not cheap. Count on about $5–$6 per person for lunch. Of course, you could always take your lunch. Then you could afford another whole outfit from the digs.

• Lynchburg—population 361—home of the Jack Daniel Distillery (931-759-6180)

It takes around an hour and a half to an hour to get there from Nashville. I suggest making the drive through Shelbyville to take in some Walking Horse country on the way. Allow seventy to ninety minutes for the free guided tour of the distillery and grounds. Your guide, usually dressed in overalls and full of fun tales and details, will take you through the same steps that have been used to make whiskey for 125 years. They also give you a peek at how the Jack Daniel beer is made.

The Jack Daniel Distillery is the nation's oldest registered distillery. There are guided tours every day from 8:00 A.M. to 4:00 P.M., except for Thanksgiving, Christmas, and New Year's Day. These tours are appropriate for the whole family. My friend Sally, who has taken dozens of groups to

Jack Daniel's, says, "It is definitely PG entertainment—only the most serious teetotaler could be offended by anything on this tour. It is really fun, with great stories and more trivia than you could imagine. There is also a nice gift shop where you can buy everything from little bitty things with Jack Daniel's logo to whole and half whiskey barrels."

At the end of the tour you get free lemonade or coffee made with the spring water that is used to make the whiskey. Another highlight of your Lynchburg visit will be lunching at Miss Mary Bobo's Boarding House. This is not cheap, but since the tour was free you might want to spring for it. It is an experience. If you want to go to Miss Mary's, it is almost essential to make a reservation several weeks in advance. You should also walk around the Lynchburg town square where you can see old-timers whittling and talking. You'll have fun browsing in the hardware store and some other quaint shops. There is a good cafe on the square, too, for lunch.

Picnic alert! You should know that, at the distillery itself, there are picnic tables situated along the creek, so if you want to bring your own, you are more than welcome. One of the beauties of Lynchburg is that you can park at the distillery and walk around the square.

It is a tiny little place with everything within walking distance. It's a real step back in time.

Other Books for Cheapos

If you haven't read enough about what to do in Nashville, there is more out there. Here are a few that I recommend:

1. *The Treasure Hunter's Guide to Historic Middle Tennessee and South Central Kentucky Antiques, Flea Markets and Junk Stores*, by Maude Gold Kiser. Published by the Gold-Kiser Company, this book features over 400 places to shop, over 170 diners and 60 bed-and-breakfast inns, as well as state resort parks. $10.95.

2. *You Don't Have to Pay Retail: Nashville's Guide to Discount Shopping*, by Paula Golomb Kirwan. This $7.95 book looks at everything from the bread stores to clothing, home furnishings, shoes, and sporting goods. Kirwan has some great ideas.

3. *Adventures in Cheap Eating: Nashville and Middle Tennessee*, by March Egerton, is a very original, opinionated guide to more than one hundred restaurants. Egerton does a great job. $9.95.

4. *Day Trips: Getaways Less Than Two Hours Away from Nashville*, by Susan Chappell. This $10.95 book takes a look at caves, battlefields, shopping, antiquing, etc. Good ideas.

5. *Nashville Inside Out: An Insider's Guide to Music City USA*, by Susan Chappell. This book is a great way to get to know Nashville. $8.95.

Bookstore Browsing

You might have noticed some mention of bookstores and related activities earlier in the book, and by now you must be aware of Ms. Cheap's appreciation for books, period. Following is a list of many of the bookstores in the Nashville area. I encourage you to seek these out if, for nothing else, than to browse, because browsing is a great and, yes, cheap way to spend an afternoon or evening, especially a rainy one:

- Baptist Book Store, 1010 Broadway, 251-2500.
- Barnes and Noble Booksellers, 1701 Mallory Lane, 377-9979.
- Best Books, 211 Donelson Pike, 883-9193.
- Bible Factory Outlet—100 Oaks Mall, 385-9045; and 2434 Music Valley Drive, 889-6467.
- Blockbuster Music—1587 Gallatin Pike North, 865-7434; The Crossing, 885-9595; 4043-B Nolensville Pike, 834-2287; and 2312 West End Avenue, 320-9788.
- Bodacious Books, 5133 Harding Pike, 356-2065.
- Book Attic, 2142 Gallatin Pike North, Madison, 859-7219.
- Book Discoveries, 2800 Bransford Avenue, 298-4800.
- The Book Gallery, 5326-A Mt. View Road, Antioch, 731-1900.
- Book Warehouse Inc., 2434 Music Valley Drive, 885-3415.
- Books-a-Million, 1789 Gallatin Pike North, 860-3133.
- Book Shop Maybe, 3736 Old Hickory Boulevard, 352-4801.
- Bookstar, 4301 Harding Road, 292-7895.
- Book Trader, 961 Richards Road, 833-9742.
- The Book Worm, 4406 Lebanon Pike, 889-8099.
- Bookman Rare and Used Books, 1724 Twenty-first Avenue South, 383-6555.
- Books at Cummins Station, 209 Tenth Avenue South, 259-2254.

- Booksearch International, 207-B Cherokee Road, 298-3804.
- Bookworld—Harding Mall, 834-1862; and 1800 Galleria Boulevard, 771-7853.
- Brentano's Bookstore, Bellevue Center, 662-1913.
- Cokesbury, 301 Eighth Avenue South, 749-6123.
- The Covenant, Rivergate Mall, Goodlettsville, 851-1521.
- Dad's Old Book Store, 4004 Hillsboro Road, 298-5880.
- Davis-Kidd Booksellers, 4007 Hillsboro Road, 385-2645.
- Doubleday Book Shop, Bellevue Center, 646-7195.
- Elder's Book Store, 2115 Elliston Place, 327-1867.
- Family Bookstores—Hickory Hollow Mall, 731-7977; Bellevue Valley Plaza, 7073 Highway 70 South, 662-2500; Cool Springs, 1800 Mallory, 370-8200; Harding Mall, 833-3600; and The Shops at Rivergate, 2162 North Gallatin Road, 851-0145.
- Franklin's Old Book Shop, 39 Public Square, Columbia, 540-0520.
- The Great Escape—1925 Broadway, 327-0646; and 111 Gallatin Pike North, 865-8052.
- J. S. Crouch Bookseller, 4714 Lebanon Pike, 316-0767.
- Logos Book and Music Center, 4012 Hillsboro Pike, 297-5388.
- Media Play—5434 Bell Forge Lane East, 731-4345; 2101 Gallatin Pike North, 851-1586; and 719 Thompson Lane, 383-5114.
- Peebles Bookstore, 360 Elysian Fields Road, 832-1577.
- Penmann Press, 5401 Meadow Lake Road, 377-3444.
- Professional Book Sellers, 2200 Twenty-first Avenue South, 383-0044.
- Saint Mary's Book Store and Church Supplies, 1909 West End Avenue, 329-1835.
- Tower Records-Video-Books, 2404 West End Avenue, 327-8085.

- Vanderbilt University Bookstore, 322-2994.
- Waldenbooks—Rivergate Mall, Goodlettsville, 859-3387; Church Street Mall, 244-9320; Paddock Place, 352-6879; and Stadium Square, Hendersonville, 824-9044.
- Winston-Derek Booksellers, 1722 West End Avenue, 329-1319.

Information Request

Ms. Cheap also suggests that you write the Nashville Area Chamber of Commerce to request a packet of information, coupon book, and a copy of the *Nashville Music City Vacation Guide*. Remember, this packet of information is as usefull for Nashville area residents as it is for tourists and business travelers. Simply fill out the following form, cut it out, and mail it to:

Nashville Area Chamber of Commerce
Convention and Visitors Bureau
161 Fourth Avenue North
Nashville, TN 37219

Dear Nashville Area Chamber of Commerce:
I have just read *Ms. Cheap's Guide to Nashville* and I would appreciate your sending me a packet of whatever promotional and informational materials you usually make available to tourists, travelers, and residents. Please include with this packet any coupon books you have available as well as the latest copy of your *Nashville Music City Vacation Guide*. Thank you for your assistance.

_____
(name)

_____
(street address)

_____
(city, state, zip code)

_____
(telephone number)